LOVE

Has No Limits

Story of Love, Loss, Betrayal, Resilience and Love Again

Arminé Papouchian

Published 2020 by Your Book Angel

Copyright © Arminé Papouchian

Printed in the United States

Edited by Keidi Keating

Layout by Rochelle Mensidor

ISBN: 978-1-7356648-1-1

Dedicated to My Parents,
Gohar and Harout Papouchian

"Love recognizes no barriers. It jumps hurdles, leaps fences, penetrates walls to arrive at its destination full of hope."

— Written by Maya Angelou

Table of Contents

Prologue

While drinking a glass of red wine, I watched the blazing fire roll down the hill. I got the second emergency alert call to evacuate immediately. I couldn't believe this was happening again. Last time this happened my son still lived at home, my parents lived with us, and Peaches, our sweet dog was still alive. Back then, I had to get everyone organized, packed, and ready to evacuate. Back then, I'd been more nervous, concerned about my aging parents, my teenage son and our dog, who could sense the tension and had anxiously paced back and forth with her tongue hanging out. This time, it was just me. I thought about what I should take with me. After all, I had already lost so much in life, yet at the same time, I felt I was blessed with all that I still had. After all, my parents had moved me halfway around the world when I was a teenager, leaving my love behind. I had grieved losing two husbands by the time I was 50, another husband in between who betrayed me at my most vulnerable moment, and I'd struggled with my father's cancer, which ended in suicide. Just as I was catching my breath, I had to put my dog to sleep followed by my mother's long-term illness and her painful death. At the same time, I was so grateful for all I had. I was so happy that I was not angry and resentful. I was not bitter; I was content. I had love again, and I was stronger than ever before. I was still standing.

As I packed a change of clothes, my laptop, few photo albums that my son requested and my small metal safe deposit box with important documents, I reflected on how little all our possessions really matter to us. As I was packing the albums, the memories started to come back, old wounds flared up and I started to feel the pain and the deep sadness. I ached for my son who had lost his father at age ten. I felt lonely; I missed the people I had in my life that I'd loved and lost. I missed all they brought to my life. At times, I could not believe I had survived all that had happened in my life in such a short time. Tears rolled down my cheeks. I realized the effects those pictures had on me and why I did not even want to take those albums with me. I had the memories in my heart and that's all I could ever have, the rest of my life. I realized that's why I no longer made photo albums. I realized how simplistic life had become for me. I did not need much. I cherished the moments I was with the people I loved and that is all I ever needed.

I put everything in my car and drove down the street and down the hill to leave Oak Park, where I had lived for 28 years. I was full of emotion. I thought this might be yet another traumatic moment in my life but at the same time, I felt like this couldn't happen. When would I ever get a break? I thought about my son and how this would affect him. After all, he and I had shared experiences and we had worked hard to always see the light. I was tired of being strong. I was tired of being in survival mode. How different my life would have been had I made different choices. I had to follow my heart. I had to live fully, not just exist in a pre-defined box. I had no regrets, as I went down my memory lane. All the events that happened in my life and choices I made shaped my life and who I am today.

Yerevan, Armenia – May, 1963

I was born in Yerevan, capital of Armenia. I always thought Yerevan was a charming city, with many parks, fountains, museums, cafes and monuments. We had all four seasons, and each had its beauty, with warm summer nights, colorful fall when leaves changed, snow in the winter, and beautiful spring when trees and flowers blossomed. My parents already had two daughters, Annie who was eight years old and Arous, who was almost eleven. They were anxiously awaited the birth of their third child, me. When my mother Gohar was in labor, my father Harout was pacing, probably secretly wishing it was a boy. In Armenia, as in many cultures, it was desirable to have a son, to carry the name and for no valid reason some people believed that's how a man proved his manhood.

Back then, no one was allowed to be with a woman during childbirth. It was not uncommon for the family to wait even outside the hospital and not be able to see their baby, except through the window—for fear of infection—until the mother and baby were discharged. Ironically, even with all that caution, most babies left the hospital with some sort of infection, mostly because the tools they used were not sterilized.

My parents had not planned for a third child but were excited to have another baby after so many years and especially with the large age difference. It was not very common to have another baby after so many years. My father was deep in thought as he watched for the door to the delivery room to open. The nurse opened the door and slowly walked toward my father with her head down, avoiding eye contact. My father got anxious, thinking that maybe something was wrong with his baby or his wife.

When the nurse walked up to him, she said, "Sir, you had a daughter." She looked away.

My dad asked, "What's wrong with my daughter? Is my wife OK?"

She said, "Yes sir, they are both doing fine."

My dad's face lit up with excitement and he walked to his chair and grabbed the bag of candy and cognac he had brought for the doctor and the nurses to hand it to her and to express his gratitude and excitement. She looked at him, surprised and said, "Sir, I think you misunderstood me, you had a daughter, not a son."

My dad said, "I know and I am very excited. I could not afford to buy a piano for my two other daughters but I am going to buy a piano for this one." She was surprised at his reaction and smiled as she walked away.

They named me Arminé, following the tradition of "A" initials for their three daughters. My oldest sister Arous (short for Arousiak, which means morning star) was named after my dad's sister, who had passed away at a very young age. My sister Annie (which is short for Anahit, the goddess of healing and wisdom) is the name of an Armenian fortress city and the queen of fertility.

Arminé is short for Armenouhi and it means a warrior woman from Armenia. My father bought me a piano and he said he never, ever regretted not having a son. He considered himself lucky being surrounded by women: his mother, sister, mother in-law, wife and three daughters, always showed him love and affection. At dinner celebrations, his first toast was always to drink to women.

My father raised us to be strong, self-reliant, educated, resilient, independent women. He always believed that education was more important for women than men and said, "I don't want my daughters to ever depend on a man or stay in an unhappy relationship for financial dependency on man. It's OK for a man to do any job but a woman needs to be educated."

My mom was one of the first and one of the very few women in Yerevan who drove a car. My father's friends always asked him if he was worried that he gave his wife too much independence, but he always said no, pointing out how she could drive him home if he'd had too much to drink. My father never told us we couldn't do something because we were girls and in fact, he encouraged us, supported us and was proud of us until the day he died. I felt so fortunate to have had a father like that and a mother who was aligned with his thinking and taught us discipline, work ethics, responsibility, and independence.

Early Years in Yerevan – 1963-1970

My parents had immigrated to Armenia, which was a part of the Soviet Union at the time, in 1946. My mom emigrated from Iraq when she was fourteen, with her widowed mother, her older sister, her uncle and his family. My father emigrated from Lebanon when he was nineteen, with his parents, brother, and sister. After the genocides, Armenians lived in many parts of the Middle East as well as other countries. Since part of Armenia at that time was already part of Turkey, many Armenians dreamt of living in their native lands. After WWII, the Soviet Union had a shortage of food, housing, and necessities, and although my parents and grandparents were happy to be in their country, they quickly realized life was very difficult and challenging. In addition, the local Armenians treated them as foreigners.

My mother's uncle was renting a house next to where my father lived. My mother often visited her uncle and her cousins, which is how my parents met in 1951. They got married in January 1952. Although my father always loved art and theatre, he was not able to make a living in that to support a family. My parents valued education, were ambitious, and were both in the first generation of their families to attend college. My father worked as a chemical engineer and oversaw an entire department. My mother was a mechanical engineer. Hardworking and financially responsible, my parents were able to own a house and a car; we often were able to go on vacations, and all our needs were met. My father would have family meetings, always allowing me and my sisters to be a part of the decision-making process. We discussed doing the labor to maintain the house ourselves so we could save for family vacations. Of course, we always agreed to do that. One year, my job was to paint the entire side fence green.

After I painted the fence solid light green, I decided that it would be nice to paint some dark green trees and flowers on it. When my parents got home from work that day, they looked at the fence and I could see the shock on their faces. My mom got angry and said she hadn't asked me to paint pictures on it, but just when she demanded I paint over it, my dad smiled and said it looked good and that we should just keep at it. I was relieved that I did not get a time out, which normally involved not being able to play outside and was always the worst punishment for me.

One of my best memories growing up was our summer vacations at the Black Sea, when we would spend a whole month in a tent on the beach, cook our meals, swim all day, and enjoy the evenings playing games, singing and dancing. Often my father would go by the fisherman in the early morning and buy fish from them for us to cook for lunch and dinner. I also loved the summer camps my parents sent me to, both Lake Sevan in Armenia and Podmoskovia, which was just outside Moscow in the forests in Russia. The only not so good part was that I was a picky eater and did not like the food there, but my grandma would come to my rescue and insist that my parents send me some of my favorite foods. Other than that, I lived on bread and cheese and apples when they had them.

One year at summer camp at Lake Sevan, my older sister Arous was a camp counselor for a boys-only group and my sister Annie was in the oldest kids group and I in the youngest kids group. Arous was able to take her group to Lake Sevan for swimming, but the girls were not allowed to go. I always begged her to sneak me in with her group but she refused because she did not want to get in trouble. Annie's group always had the opportunity to play ping-pong and they didn't allow the younger kids to play but I always wanted to play and knew how to play because we had a ping-pong table on our veranda at home. One time I stole the ping-pong ball when they were playing and jumped out the window. That day, during the evening flag ceremony, I was reprimanded while Annie was being praised because she had done such a good job helping in the kitchen with the potatoes. One would wonder if we were even sisters at all as I always got in trouble and Annie was always the most loved and praised, at school, at camp, at home, everywhere.

I had a happy childhood. I was always surrounded by family, and I felt loved. Even when we did not have a lot, we were content. I was just as content when my mom made our clothes as I am now having beautiful store-bought clothes and shoes. It was enough and we were grateful with what we had. Material things never defined us. My father always considered himself a "rich" man because he had a beautiful family; he considered that to be his fortune.

My maternal grandmother lived with us and she was always very warm and attentive. I was not a very good eater, and some days it felt that her only goal was to chase me and try to get me to eat something. I loved my grandmother and felt awfully close to her. She was very loving and protective of me and she often took me with her when she visited her friend who lived down the street. My grandma lived a difficult life. She was a genocide survivor, she walked the migration when she was only twelve and had difficult memories to share with us. She also immigrated to Armenia on a boat as a single parent with her two daughters and worked at the cigarette factory in Soviet Armenia to provide for her children. Even having lost a husband at very young age and two children who passed away at very young ages due to illness, her heart was full of love. I never met my maternal grandfather. He died when my mom was only two. My paternal grandparents, along with my uncle Stepan and his family, lived upstairs on the second floor. We often had family visiting us, or we visited them. We lived in a safe neighborhood where kids could play outside and everyone knew everyone else, making it safe to walk most places.

From an early age, I was independent, active, curious and strong-willed at times. I loved playing outside with my friends and dreaded being called in for dinner. I even once ran away from pre-school when I was only four. I'd gone to the barbershop where my grandpa got his haircut. I enjoyed talking to all the barbers and ran away from pre-school because they were forcing me to eat food that I did not like. My pre-school was at the end of my street and my parents usually dropped me off on their way to work in the mornings, but pretty soon I started walking to pre-school alone, and I would meet up with friends once I arrived. One of the girls on our street did not know how to tie her shoes. Every morning, she would wait for me to help her tie her shoe and then she would walk with me to pre-school. Even at pre-school, I loved playing outside and had a hard time when it was naptime.

The summers were always fun even when we were just home, with longer days to play outside, going on vacations, and long weekends going out of town for picnics and camping. My mom always insisted on having a schedule in the summer and she would ask me to prepare one: when I was going to get up, exercise, eat, read, play outside, do my chores, etc. Then she would always change it because she believed I allocated too much playtime for outside and at times, it would become a negotiation. My grandma never told my parents when I played outside longer than I was supposed to because she did not want me to get in trouble.

At age seven, as I got closer to starting first grade, as promised, my father bought me a piano, so I could start piano lessons at the music school. As excited as I had been about it, I knew I would have less playtime outside because I would have to practice daily. I was more excited to learn how to ride a two-wheel bicycle on my street and pretty soon I was the official messenger for my family, using my bicycle to take all the shoes that needed repair to the shoemaker as well as run other errands. At times, I sat with the shoemaker in his white booth while he repaired the shoes and talked about recent events in the neighborhood. Sometimes, when I bought something from the store for my mom or my grandma or my sisters, I would visit one of my friends in another neighborhood.

Since I was the only one in my family who could not swim, the first time we went to the Black Sea, my parents signed me up for the swim team. I enjoyed swimming, except when we had to do laps in the outdoor pool while it was snowing. It was so cold and I would ask the coach if I could go inside for few minutes and warm up in the hot shower but my coach would always say: "If you keep swimming, you won't feel cold, keep going."

The winters were all about ice-skating, hockey and sledding. I remember when I had gotten comfortable with two blade training skates, my father and I went to buy regular skates and I wanted black ones instead of white ones so I could play hockey with the boys in my neighborhood and not stand out as a girl. My dad asked me, "Why don't you want the white ones? The black ones are boys' skates." Once I explained to him he indulged me with a smile but reminded me to be careful as my grandma always worried when I played hockey, fearing I would lose my teeth if I got hit by the hockey puck.

Carefree Years – 1970s

I started school when I was seven years old. In Armenia, you start first grade at age seven and back then school lasted ten years. The schools in Armenia were not separated into elementary school, middle school, and high school. It was all one school. I went to the same school as my sister Annie and when I started first grade, she was in ninth grade at the same school. One of my cousins, who was only a year older and shared my surname, also went to the same school. Although it was nice having my sister and my cousin in the same school, it was also frustrating. Whenever I started with a new teacher, based on my surname, they would always compare me to my sister or my cousin. I was different in some ways, especially our personalities. My sister was very quiet and all the teachers loved her so whenever I was too talkative in class, my teachers would reprimand me, expecting me to be quiet too.

Even though it was for a short time, I liked having my sister Annie in the same school. I sometimes visited her classroom during recess and her friends were always very nice to me and played with me by chasing me around and steeling my hand-knit white beret I used to wear to school. Annie often took me to plays or symphonies or ballets when she went with her school friends, which I always enjoyed.

I met Alex in first grade. He was in my class. He always came to school with clean clothes and nicely brushed hair. He spoke Armenian with a Russian—his native language—accent. Before moving to Armenia, he had lived in Turkmenistan, another Soviet Republic, most of his life. In Armenia, you stayed with the same classmates for the entire ten years of school.

Throughout my school years, I was involved in many extracurricular activates, such as piano, art, swimming, fencing, dancing, and drama. I enjoyed school and all of the activities, except piano. I dreaded practicing and always excused myself to go to the bathroom during practice just to kill some time. My piano teacher was very strict and almost mean, so that did not help. My school and all my extracurricular activities were either within walking distance or a bus stop away. I enjoyed walking to school and walking home with my friends and in general the independence of being able to go where I needed to go, including visiting friends or relatives. I also loved going to the movies or to the park with friends, hosting or going to house parties where we danced and enjoyed great music in different languages—French, Italian, Spanish in addition to Armenian and Russian, and we loved many American and European bands. I always enjoyed the house parties as my parents hosted parties and my sisters did with their friends too. I was thankful that my sisters let me stay when they had parties and let me dance with their friends, even though they were so much older than me. In return, they would send me to the basement or to the store to get stuff for them and one day when I got tired of doing that, I told them when they had kids, I was going to do the same to their kids. I never got the chance as we moved before their kids were old enough to reciprocate for me.

By far though, my ultimate favorite thing to do was to play outside and whenever I got sick, which seemed often with earaches, mumps, measles, chicken pox and often sore throat with high fevers, I was not allowed to go to school or play outside. I sat by the window facing the front street and watched my friends play or I talked to them through the window. And when I got high fevers, the doctor would make a house call, and at some point, my parents decided I needed to have a tonsillectomy because I got sick too often. However, because of the fear of infection at the hospitals, my parents hired a private doctor to perform the tonsillectomy at home, in our kitchen. I think the local anesthesia had worn off by the time she finished cutting out one of them because the second one was so painful that my neighbors heard my scream and came over wondering what was going on. I could not eat or even swallow my spit initially until I started drinking some water with a straw. My grandma was always very compassionate and made chicken noodle soup for me and pealed tangerines whenever I was sick and took good care of me. I was so mad at my parents for making me go through that at home, but after my tonsils were removed, I rarely had the high fevers any longer.

Over the years, Alex and I developed a really close friendship. We had many interests in common. I was on a swim team and he was on a diving team, he was my dance partner in the school dance group, he and I were the leads in several Shakespeare plays like *Romeo and Juliet* and *Othello*. We also both liked Russian poetry and easily memorized and recited many that we enjoyed by Lermontov and Pushkin. He was a spirited person similar to me where we liked being outdoors and walking long stretches or dancing non-stop at parties. It was probably eighth grade when I noticed that he liked me as more than a friend, although he claimed that he'd had a crush on me since fifth grade. He was always such a good friend to me that I had a hard time seeing him as anything other than a really good friend.

Our school had three eighth grade classes. However, some kids had changed schools or dropped out so going into ninth grade, they split our class so the school ended up with only two ninth grade classes. Alex and I were split up. Although some of our same classmates were with us in our new respective classes, there were a lot of new kids we both had to connect with and make friends with. I was actually excited to be in the class I was because there was a boy in that class, Sam, that I had a crush on and now I got to be in the same class as him every day, every period. The house parties we had usually only included fellow classmates. When the new kids arrived, the dynamics changed. There was no one in the new class that liked dancing as much as me or danced as well as Alex. I missed my dance partner. He felt the same way. Some classmates were jealous about us dancing together, so we had to change partners. Sometimes we would ask permission from our classmates for me to go to Alex's class house parties and for him to come to my class house parties and even with that, it just was not the same. We sort of drifted apart as friends in the ninth grade, saw each other less and spent less time with each other naturally since we were not in the same class. I was interested in spending more time with Sam and was dancing with him more or participating in activities where he was going to be. Although Alex and I were not romantically involved, I realized that I liked spending time with Alex more than Sam, because Sam just was not very interesting although he was really handsome, with ash blond hair and blue eyes, and when he wore his turquoise blue velvet jacket with his tight jeans, his eyes looked the same color as his jacket. By the end of ninth grade, I had lost complete interest in Sam.

In the meantime, my sisters had both gotten married and my niece Esther was born in 1977 and my nephew Tony in 1978. I loved them and enjoyed when they visited or spent the night and always wanted to spend time with them. Tony was shy, sweet, and very attached to his mom. Although he would play and interact when we were at home, he would not want to go outside or visit my friends with me. Esther was very active and was more willing so I would take her on walks in a stroller or we would go visit my friends. At a very young age, she liked music and dancing. I would get her to dance with my friends and me and had the opportunity to expose her to a lot of '60s and '70s music. I was one of the few people in my age group who had a niece and a nephew, except Alex had a nephew who was the same age as my niece so we would compare our experiences. He, too, loved playing with kids just as I did.

It was October 7th, 1979, I was in tenth grade, my last year of high school. My mom had asked me to go to the post office to mail a telegram. I asked my girlfriend Vartuk if she would go with me. It was a sunny and pleasant day and we talked and laughed and as we walked to the post office. I mailed the telegram and as we walked back from the post office, Alex and Serge walked toward us from the opposite direction. Serge was a year older than us but part of our circle of friends and we often spent time at his house after school as he lived right across the street from our school. I remember his mom did not work and she was always very warm and welcoming and often prepared meals for us. We stopped to talk to them and soon in the conversation, Alex and I started talking about Tolstoy's *Anna Karenina*. I guess we got too deep into the conversation for our friends and they both said that they had to get home. Alex and I continued to talk and soon I realized that I needed to get home too. He asked, "Can I walk with you and we can continue the discussion?" I agreed. As we got to my house, he asked if I would like to go to the zoo with him one day next week after school. I accepted his invitation and we agreed to meet at the bus stop after school on Tuesday. He commented on how it would be a lovely day, which would inspire me to paint. He knew I loved art and painting. He always complimented my paintings. I went home and he walked toward the bus stop. That evening, I realized I really missed his friendship and companionship and I was looking forward to spending more time with him again. For the first time, I realized that I was interested in more than friendship with him and that is how everything started.

Seven-Month Romance
– October 1979–May 1980

On Tuesday, October 9th, 1979, Alex and I took the bus after school to go to the zoo. It was a beautiful fall day as Alex had expected. We walked around, watched the animals and tried to identify with them. He thought he was more like a tiger and I was more like a panther and made jokes comparing our personalities. We then ran over the dried leaves and admired the fall colors of the trees as we talked about poetry, music, art and nature. We were in our last year of high school, so we also talked about what we wanted to do after graduation. We wished we could go live in Spain and go to school there but we knew that was an unrealistic dream. We both enjoyed works of Dumas, Balzac, Cervantes, and Voltaire and often got into discussions regarding works of great philosophers like Aristotle, Plato, Socrates and contemplated studying literature or philosophy. We talked about leaving Yerevan and going to school somewhere in Russian, away from our routines with the wanderlust of wanting to seek new experiences and be independent. We had this romantic notion that being away would be something wonderful and make us feel like we were adults.

Soon we found a bench and sat, still having a very engaging conversation and I realized that I saw him differently. Not only was he a good friend and not only did we have so much in common in how we thought about things, but there was also a deeper connection. At some point he had his arm around my shoulder, and he kissed me ever so gently and when I did not resist, he kissed me again and much deeper. As I felt the butterflies in my stomach and felt my heart pump, I realized everything between us had changed. He pulled away and said to me, "Do you know how long I have wanted to do that?" That's when we started talking, sharing our thoughts and feelings and realizing that we had this amazing chemistry all along: when we danced, when we were in plays, when we were having passionate discussion or sharing favorite lines from poetry, but it was kind of tucked away in fear of losing our friendship. From that day on, Alex and I were together every opportunity we had. He would even sometimes skip his class and come sit in my class just to be in the same class with me, which was not something that was allowed but somehow, he got away with it. We went to each other's class house parties and we were even better dancers than before with all the fire and chemistry between us. We were so hungry for intimacy and looked for opportunities to be alone to kiss and touch and be physically close but it was not easy to find those opportunities. It was not acceptable by our cultures to have a sexual relationship until marriage and we were too young. We were also young and naive about it. There was no sex education at school nor did our parents have those types of conversations with us.

Then one day, in early 1980, the realization came that my family was in fact going to leave Armenia and move to the Unites States. Although I knew all along that my parents wanted to do that, I had been in denial and didn't think it would happen very soon or I refused to think about it. After all, it had been several years since we applied and we still did not have permission to leave the country. Many people applied to leave and most of them got denied so I never thought that day would actually come. One day I just started hearing conversations at home that we had permission to leave but we had to keep that information confidential, as my parents did not want any ill-willing people to interfere with our plans. If someone went to the government and told them that my parents owed them money or we added a room to our house without a permit or any other reason, the government could stop us from going, even if it was not true.

My parents started to discuss what we could and would take with us or leave behind. They decided not to sell our house, our car or any of our furniture or many of our possessions so that no one would suspect we had permission and we were getting ready to leave. Only close family and friends knew and no one even knew the exact date we will be leaving. Although I was probably too young to comprehend all that and understand the impact of it all, I felt anxious and nervous yet at the same time, selfishly, I was thinking about Alex and myself and our relationship. What was going to happen to us? We would no longer be at school together. What about our love, our friendship, our dreams of being together forever? He begged me not to go with my parents, but that was impossible. You had to be eighteen to be able to make that choice. What was amazing was that here we had gone to school together for almost ten years, and only the last seven months before I left we realized this amazing connection. Why had we wasted all this time? What were we going to do? We both felt that we could not be without each other and we had to come up with a plan to reunite. We were so in love, but we were also so sad and heart-broken.

Less than a month before my departure, we had a horrendous tragedy in our class. One of our classmates committed suicide by jumping out of the window of their apartment, from the ninth floor. Later we found out she had been pregnant. It was unacceptable for a sixteen-year-old to get pregnant in Armenia. Although we did not know for sure as no one really talked about it or shared any details, we could only assume she could not bear to tell her parents. She came from a very conservative family and she was the oldest of the four girls. Our entire class was traumatized by the event, as we went to pay our condolences to her family and attended the funeral the next day. Our entire classed worked for hours to cover her burial site with red and white carnations by hand. I don't know if the schools in Armenia have it now, but back then, there were no counselors to manage the trauma, teachers and administrators just did not even talk about it and there was no forum to allow the kids to express themselves. It was a very difficult time for our class, right before graduating high school. We felt the sadness of losing a classmate at a very young age by suicide for a long time and it was difficult not to cry for days and weeks afterward when we were at school, remembering her.

The day finally arrived. I turned seventeen on May 6, 1980 and we were leaving the next day, May 7th, exactly seven months after Alex's and my random meeting on the street on the way back from the post office. I had a birthday party and then I begged my parents to allow me to spend my last night with my friends, including Alex, just walking around the city, parks, and fountains, having meals at the cafes and whatever else we felt like doing. For my birthday, Alex gave me a silver promise ring with an amethyst stone that I still have. I treasured that ring as my most valued possession. When you are a teenager, your friends are everything to you, especially when you are moving halfway around the world and have no idea if you will ever see them again. Spending that last night with my friends meant a lot to me.

My sisters and their families were not coming with us; they did not have permission because they were considered separate families since they were married and had their children. Part of me felt guilty that I wanted to be with my friends on my last night and not my sisters, but when you are seventeen and your sisters are twenty-five and twenty-seven, married with kids already, right or wrong, being with your friends and the love of your life feels more enticing. Besides, the plan was for us to send my sisters and their families the necessary documents for them to apply to move to US as well, so I knew I would see them and at that time, I thought that was going to be very soon. I promised my parents that I would meet them at the airport in the morning. Surprisingly, my father agreed, but my mother did not like the idea and was worried that I would not show up. My father assured her that I would show up. He was more willing to take the risk because he knew me better or trusted me more. It was almost because he trusted me that I could not let him down, and I had to show up. My dad was a man of his word and I knew the importance of keeping a promise.

My friends, Alex and I spend the whole night together just walking around in Yerevan, going to cafes and parks, talking, crying, reminiscing, imagining the future, promising to write letters. There was no Internet connection for emails back then. Alex and I decide that we were both going to continue our education for one year and when I was eighteen, I was going to come back and we were going to get married and go to school together in Russia. As the sun started rising, we all started to head over to the airport. All my friends skipped school that day. One of our friends was taking pictures when we were all at the airport and later my friend Vartuk sent me some of those black and white pictures. You could tell how sad everyone looked and how tired everyone was from staying up all night.

My parents were relieved to see that I showed up. Part of me felt guilty that my sisters could not be at the airport but my friends were. I remember it was a sunny beautiful day, with a light breeze. There were some fields by the airport and the poppies were blooming at that time and with the breeze, it looked like waves of beautiful, red field poppies. Alex picked a few and gave them to me, along with a small dancer he had carved out of wood and a poem he had written for me as a parting gift. Alex and I were very emotional, and I felt guilty that I did not have any last minute parting gift although few weeks prior, I had given him one of my paintings. It was of a summerhouse by the mountains with the trees and flowers out front and I had named it "Our Summer House." I never would've imagined that he would keep that painting for many years to come. As I went through customs not knowing when or if I would ever see him, I waved back. I walked on the tarmac toward the plane, and I realized that I did have one last present I wanted to give him. I had my diary of seven months that I had started on October 7th, 1979. Although it was very private and intimate, I did not care if he read my inner most feelings and thoughts. I ran back toward the fence as the border patrol had their eyes on me and were wondering what was going on. I was able to squeeze the small diary through the fence, touching his fingers one more time before I ran back to join my parents. He asked me, "What is this?"

I said, "It's my diary. Keep it until me meet again next year." How was I to know that I would get it back 31 years later?

Sad Times in Lebanon – 1980

Although we had a relatively good life in Armenia, my mom was always very frustrated with the system, with the bribery and corruption, with the constant shortage of goods, with always having to know people and having to bribe them to get basic things. I think what broke the camel's back was when my oldest sister graduated as an engineer, and although she was very qualified, she did not get the job she wanted because she was a daughter of "aghpar"—an Armenian who was not born in Armenia. It took a lot of persuasion on my mom's part, but she finally convinced my dad that we needed to leave the country and move to the US where their daughters would have better opportunities and would not have to go through the same challenges they were going through to raise their families.

My father worked for a company that made printed circuit boards for aircraft and his job and the company was considered classified. For him to apply to leave the country, he could no longer work there. So he left his very successful job managing several hundred employees and got a job as the person in charge of all photo and recording studios in Yerevan. He only got that job because of his connections. Not only he had to leave his job, but he also had to be out of his job for a few years before we could actually leave. My parents made great sacrifices for their children. They left a comfortable life, my dad at the age of 53 and my mom at the age of 48, to move half way around the world, to start a new life, to learn a new language, to start from nothing just for the future of their children. After several years of waiting for permission to leave the country, with the help of a friend who had a connection at the immigration office and with bribery, which I learned about years later, we were allowed to leave the country and go to Lebanon. Since my father was originally from Lebanon, my parents thought that through his friends and connections, we would be able to get our visas from the American Embassy to move to the US. However, it was 1980, the American Marines were in Lebanon, there was a war and the American Embassy was often closed and it was very difficult to get anything done. Sometimes traveling from one part of town to the other, we weren't sure if we should even show our Russian passports at check points because of safety issues. When we left Armenia, we were only allowed to take one suitcase each, a few hundred dollars and no jewelry or anything of value. My parents were allowed to take only their wedding bands. My father had been able to transfer some money ahead of time—over the years while we were waiting for our permission—through some friends and relatives from Lebanon who would visit us in Armenia. He would offer them a certain percentage to transfer it. That was the only way we could have some money when we got there. There were no written contracts, you simply had to trust people and although most came through with their promises and paid my father his portion, some did not.

When we were in Beirut, Lebanon, we didn't know how long we would be there and basically had only our clothes. We rented an apartment in a five-story building, on the top floor, where our ceiling had been repaired from bomb damage. At the entrance of the building, there were always armed soldiers for security reasons, which was not something we were used to, and it felt unnerving at times. For people who lived in Beirut, that was normal. They just went on with their lives, worked, went shopping and went to restaurants, celebrated, had weddings and births and almost ignored the fact that they were in war. After some time though, we even got used to it. I felt comfortable going by myself to get fresh boreg (cheese bread) or ice cream from around the building.

There were mostly small stores on the first floor of the buildings and often we could just drop a bag with a rope from our balcony with a list of a few grocery items. The grocery store owners would put the groceries in the bag with the bill and we would pull it up. We would then send down the money we owed in the bag. Beirut was a noisy city, with lots of traffic, people on the streets, store owners shouting loudly to invite customers in, all the taxis were Mercedes with a variety of musical horns, and there were armed soldiers everywhere. It felt like organized chaos.

Even though we lived in Bourj Hamoud, which is the Armenian neighborhood of Beirut, the culture was very different. I grew up with Russian influence and the Armenians in Beirut had Middle Eastern influence. Although they had the freedom to travel wherever they wanted to, similar educational opportunities, an abundance of goods and services available to them, in some ways, they were not as progressive in their thinking when it came to women's education or women's roles in the society. Even a seventeen-year-old like me felt the difference and did not necessarily like it. Many of my father's friends were trying to convince us to stay there, with the promise that once the war was over, things would be good, his friends would help him start some sort of small business and his wife and daughter could stay home. Although Lebanon was a beautiful country, with the Mediterranean Sea on one side and mountains on another, and although Beirut was a lively, and in some ways a very European city, neither my mother nor I wanted to live there. My mom was very set on her goal and she wanted to get to her destiny so she could bring her other daughters and Lebanon was not where she thought her daughters would have the best opportunity. I could not see myself missing out on my education or getting married young to someone with very different values and beliefs and just being a housewife. I saw that most women spent their days shopping, having coffee with their friends, cooking for their husbands, and attending to their children's needs, while men just went to work. Most of them were very happy with their roles and the lifestyle they chose. It just was not the desired lifestyle for my mom or me, nor did I think it would be to my sisters' liking. We were raised to value education and pursue professional aspirations and my mom had been a great role model for us.

After some time, we realized that we were not going to get our visas in Lebanon because of the war situation and we found out that in Italy, there was an organization called VCC, which was a world church organization that helped people from socialist countries immigrate to the US, Canada or Australia. We got our tickets and flew to Rome from Beirut with the hopes of getting our visas to go to the US through this organization. While we were in Lebanon, Alex and I had not been able to correspond at all, except the one letter I got from him through one of my father's friends who was traveling from Armenia to Iraq through Lebanon. I was excited when I received that letter, and I read it over and over. And now, we were moving to Italy and once again I did not know how long we were going to stay there and when I will be able to correspond with him again. I was missing him so much. I was in a constant state of sadness and nothing and no one could make me smile or make me feel excited even with all the abundance of goods we had access to in Beirut that we had lacked in Yerevan. I did not care. I wanted to go back.

Italy – Pasta and Pizza and More Waiting

We arrived in Italy and found out that there were many Armenians and Russian Jews who were all staying at this particular hostel in Rome, very close to the VCC office. The hostel had very basic, low-cost accommodations and common areas for eating, cafeteria style. The food was included with the room and we quickly discovered that they served three meals a day and all three times it was a variation of pasta. My dad would not eat pasta for a long time after we left that place. There were some other families there too, all from socialist countries, all waiting for their visas to go to the US, Canada or Australia. We walked to the VCC office every day or sometimes every other day, hoping we would get our visas. On our way there, we would pass by Alpha Romeo car dealership and I remember admiring the beauty and the design of the cars. They looked so much prettier than the cars I was used to seeing in Armenia. My dad was exploring to see if bribery would work at the VCC office the same way it worked in the Soviet Union with no success. They were getting tired of seeing us at the office and at some point, they suggested we should consider going to Canada or Australia because the wait was much shorter, but my parents were set on the US. I just wanted to get someplace permanent so I could get on with my life and be able to correspond with Alex.

There were other families with children my age and we would all gather in front of the hostel and commiserate. We had no money to do anything, except get ice cream occasionally, we did not speak the language and we did not know anyone there. Occasionally, the hostel's owner's son, who had a Vespa, would give me a ride to a coffee place or to get ice cream and that helped with the monotony of just waiting around, but communication was challenging and frustrating. Not knowing how long it would take to get our visas was the worst part.

At some point my parents decided that since we are waiting anyway and we didn't know when we would ever return to Italy, we should see the country. One of the young men in his late twenties, whose family had been waiting there longer than us, had started to pick up some Italian and was organizing big bus tours at a very reasonable price for all of us waiting for our visas. We got to see Venice; we got to see Florence, the Tower of Pisa, Sienna and many smaller towns.

After about a month or so, a Jewish family who had a son around my age, asked my parents if we wanted to share a small apartment in Lido de Ostia, a beach town about 25 miles from Rome. My parents agreed and we left the hostel and moved to Lido de Ostia. The apartment was walking distance to the beach, the Mediterranean Sea. We shared the bathroom, the kitchen, our meals and any common areas and enjoyed the relaxing atmosphere of this beautiful beach town and it cost us less than the hostel. We also learned about pizza and to this date, sometimes I think that was the best pizza I'd ever had in my life, despite having been back to Italy many times. Their son Michael and I sometimes walked to the beach, and put our change together to buy one small pizza to share. That was considered indulgence for us. We also learned about Amaretto and my mom and I took to the liking. Sometimes we drank too much and cried, my mom for missing my sisters and me for missing Alex.

Even though it was a beautiful beach town, after a couple of weeks, I just wanted to leave, I wanted to go back to Yerevan, I wanted to go somewhere permanent, I wanted to get on with my life. The uncertainty was very difficult, and it was even more difficult and nerve-wracking for my parents. They had their daughters that they still had to worry about and felt responsible for. We had limited resources and still had expenses to cover once we got to the US, not knowing where we were going to live, what jobs could we have, what school I would go to, how long would it take for my sisters to join us or how we would support them once they got to the US. I often daydreamed about my life in Yerevan, about my friends, about Alex and I knew that things would never be the same. Every few days we would take the train to Rome to check on the status, and often return disappointed with no news and it got harder and harder to wait, to hope, to think positive. Sometimes we would just call instead of going there by train to save money.

I swam in the Mediterranean Sea every day. I would look beyond the horizon and wonder what was next, how long we would be in this situation, what Alex was doing, whether he was thinking of me or wondering if I had forgotten about him. When I looked at the sea, I often thought of a Russian poem that I had learned when I was young about a lonely white sailboat in a distance, in the blue waters, wondering what it was looking for or what it had lost in deep waters and at times I felt like I was that lonely sailboat, wondering what life was going to bring next. Since I had left a month before graduation, I had missed the prom and all the summer entrance exams for University, which I did not mind. I had no idea where my friends were going to school or if some were getting married or where Alex was going to move.

In late July, the family we were sharing the apartment with got their visas to go to Australia. They were so excited. Their daughter, son-in-law and granddaughter lived there, and they could not wait to reunite with them. We were just getting adapted to the uncertainty and trying to make the best of it, and this good news gave us new hope. A few days later, we went to Rome and my father went inside the VCC office to speak with the lady who was in charge of this whole process. My mom and I waited outside, expecting no news again and were thinking of walking by the hostel to see some of the people we had become friends with and to see if anyone else had news about their visa status. My father took longer than expected. It was early August and very hot as we waited outside. All of a sudden, he walked out with some papers and my mom thought that they needed us to complete more forms and we would need someone to help us, since the forms were all in Italian. As my father walked toward us, I noticed that he was walking faster and seemed excited, almost like he was trying to contain his excitement but was having a hard time doing so. Sure enough, we had gotten our visas; we had our permission to go to the US. All we had to do was pack and get our airline tickets.

The next day, we went to the Pan Am office to get our tickets from Rome to New York City, where my mom had a cousin and we could initially stay with her. A few days later, we were on the plane, on our way to New York, with new hope, renewed energy and excitement and with apprehension at the same time. Although this was not my first time on an airplane, it was going to be my longest flight. We were actually going to cross the Atlantic Ocean, which was fascinating to me since I always loved geography. I had never actually seen an ocean and now I was going to see one on our way to New York, and I was going to be on another continent. I felt we were finally going to have some stability and start our new life. Also, I could start corresponding with Alex on a regular basis. Somehow, that made me feel closer to our reunification date even though we were now further apart.

We arrived in New York in August of 1980. My mom's cousin's family met us at the airport and drove us to their apartment in Queens. Everything looked new and different—the large American cars, the multi-cultural and multi-racial population, the large roads, buildings, supermarkets, the language, the traffic, the noise, the dirty streets, homeless people, billboards, the humidity and so much more. It was all overwhelming and hard to take in. Their old apartment building in Queens had marble floors and an old-fashion elevator; but they had an amazing view of the Manhattan skyline from the kitchen window of their tiny apartment. We spent the next week sleeping in their living room, learning some basics about the culture, constantly sweating from the heat and humidity and taking three showers a day. After a week, my parents decided that they did not want to live in New York and went to buy airline tickets to go to Los Angeles, where my parents had a godson and one of my cousins on my mom's side. As much as I hated the heat and humidity in New York, I thought to myself, "When are we ever going to get someplace where we can settle?" I hoped Los Angeles was our last stop, at least for a while, at least until I was eighteen so I could go back and be with Alex.

Los Angeles, Here We Come

We arrived in Los Angeles and got situated with my parents' godson Varouj until we found an apartment. When we landed and as Varouj drove us to their apartment, Los Angeles looked very different from New York. It did not look like a city and I was surprised, unimpressed and disappointed by the look of it. They lived in Glendale, which was considered part of Los Angeles, and everything felt so spread out and distant. There were no people on the streets, no metro, not much public transportation, no cafes, no monuments, no high-rise building, no fountains or large parks and you needed to have a car to get anywhere. Unfortunately, our luggage did not arrive with us and we did not have even any change of clothes for a few days. We had to borrow a few things and wash and re-wear the same clothes until we got our luggage. We did get a small apartment near them in Glendale. I enrolled in Glendale High School and my parent and I attended language school.

When we went to the school to enroll, they asked me what classes I wanted to take. I was surprised to have a choice as in

Armenia, I was used to a uniform mandatory curriculum that everyone went through. My parents also started looking for jobs, which proved to be a very difficult with limited language and no experience in this country. My mother quickly decided that she would go to trade school and learn accounting, which would take a few months. That ended up being a good decision for her as she was able to find a job when she finished the program. For my father, it was impossible to get a job as an engineer. He was willing to do any work just to earn some money. He ended up getting a silk-screening job, driving over 30 miles each way. He often worked overtime to make more money. The job was physically demanding and I could see the toll it took on him. He would get up very early, take his lunch with him and come home exhausted. He slept on the sleeper sofa in the living room and let my mom and I sleep on the bed in the bedroom so that he wouldn't wake us up in the mornings.

I felt out of place in high school, not knowing the language, struggling with my grades, not having any friends, and often wondering what would become of me. It's not uncommon for teenagers to be very selfish and not have the patience to interact with anyone who did not speak English or make an effort to understand an accent. However, that experience taught me to turn on my hearing a notch when I tried to understand what they were saying and to this day, I understand people with accents much better than most Americans who don't speak any other language, and I am particularly sensitive to people with accents and speak slowly so they understand me. The school system was very different. I had the option to choose certain classes and had language not been a barrier for me, I would have felt that it was not very challenging compared to what I was used to.

By late August, Alex had already moved to Sverdlovsk and, as a student in the Soviet Era, could not easily have any direct correspondence with anyone from the US. We started corresponding through my friend Vartuk in Yerevan. I would send my letters to her, she would forward them to Alex and Alex would send his letter to my friend and she would forward them to me. It took a long time to get our letters back and forth. In the meantime, he had started at the University and seemed to enjoy being in Sverdlovsk. Our letters were heartwarming, sometimes sad, and sometimes happy, but the distance wore down our seventeen-year-old hearts. Pretty soon, I was going to be eighteen and I had promised to go back. I started to have second thoughts.

I felt a deep sense of responsibility for my parents. I could not be yet another burden for them and add to their worries by moving back. Having had to move at age seventeen and needing to worry about school and work had expedited my adulthood and it felt like I was missing out the most fun and carefree part of my youth at times. But sometimes you don't realize what you are missing, until it has passed you already. I learned to live in this country; I adjusted, and I could see the potential for my future in this country compared to the Soviet Union. I was so young to make that kind of life-changing decision. I struggled with the decision for a while. Part of me was feeling that Alex and I had overcome the separation of one year and now we could finally be together, which is something we kept writing about, dreaming about and planning for and we could not wait for that time to come. Part of me was realizing and seeing what my parents had hoped for in terms of opportunities for their children: the standard of living in the US, educational opportunities, career opportunities, financial independence, equality in a sense that if you worked, you could provide for yourself and you could have your basic needs met without corruption or bribery. How could I just throw all that away? I was the fortunate one and the privileged one to reap the benefits while my sisters were still struggling and were tenaciously pursuing their plans to come to the US. What if I ended up being the only one here and if I go back, will that destroy my parents' hopes and dreams? My parents had risked all they had worked for over about 30 years and had leaped into an unknown future with no guarantees of jobs and with uncertainty of life in a new country half way around the world with language challenges and at their age. I had great appreciation for it. I didn't even sense that they had any fear and maybe they did but their courage and desire to give their children a better opportunity in life was even greater. I could not even comprehend if that was something I could ever do.

I decided that I needed to approach the subject with Alex and be honest with him. It was really hard to have that conversation with letters that took so long to go back and forth, but I had no choice. In my letter, I basically explained to him that we were too young to make that kind of decision and that we should both continue with our studies and see where life brought us. I also suggested that we remain friends and write to each other. He did not like my letter. He told me later that he tore it and burned it. He did write me back saying that he was disappointed, but he had expected that I would not go back, and it would be too hard for him to be just friends. He also said he was not surprised how quickly capitalism had changed me, which hurt me. My decision was not about capitalism, it was about necessity and a sense of responsibility I felt toward my parents. I tried writing him back to continue the conversation, to explain the opportunities I had here and the sense of responsibility I felt toward my family, to pursue at least friendship and perhaps explore other options for our future to keep the door open, but he did not respond. I waited for months and when he did not write back, I knew it was over. I was devastated, ending just like that, not ever communicating with the person I was so in love with. He meant the world to me and how could life be so cruel to two people who loved each other so much. Would I regret my decision? Would I ever find anyone like him? If he had expected me to not go back, had he really loved me or was this just a way out for him so he could continue with his life? After all, why would he want to commit to me at such a young age when he had his whole life in front of him, his college years, new friends and new girls in Sverdlovsk, beautiful Russian girls who would take him with open arms?

I had mixed feelings but, at the same time, I just could not see myself going back when I saw how my sisters being so far away affected my parents. I was their only daughter with them, and not knowing how long it would take for my sisters to come to the US, I couldn't just leave my parents and go back. How could one year make such a difference in my thinking? Perhaps it was a true love, but I chose to stay instead of going back to be with my love. How could I do that to my parents? They left everything and sacrificed their life to come to US to give their daughters better opportunity in life. I kept thinking; what if my sisters could not come? That fear was always in my mind. Although I believed I truly loved Alex and felt like I was losing the greatest love of my life at that time, I chose to stay and lose my love. How little did I know what the future held for me: love, loss, resilience, betrayal and love again.

I soon realized that I could not possibly take all the required classes in one year to graduate from high school. It was almost ridiculous to think that even though I had five years of physics, four years of chemistry, calculus, geography, several history classes and many other literature and language classes in Armenian and Russian, I could not graduate because I needed US history, health education and several years of English to graduate. My only other option to continue my education was to go to community college and transfer. I was happy I had an option. We also realized that going to college costs money in the US when in Armenia, you received a stipend. It was difficult financially already because my parents were not making much money; we were still trying to help my sisters in Armenia and also save money. I told my parents that I could work full time and help them financially instead of going to school, but my parents would not have it. I even considered joining the Marines because they would pay for my schooling, until the recruiters showed up at my house without me notifying my parents. My parents got very upset with me and were adamantly against me joining the Marines. I decided to just work full time in the summers and part time during school to pay for my school and help with some of the expenses.

We lived very frugally, shopped at the $5 store, never ate out and I even utilized K-Mart's layaway plan if I wanted to buy something and pay $5 toward it every month until I could have it. With all that, we were content. I never felt poor. We were in a completely new country with a new language, we had jobs, we did not need to rely on anyone, we had food, we had a roof over our heads, and we did not deal with bribery and corruption to get anything done. There were rules and laws and that gave us peace and gratitude. In a short time, we were here and we were making progress.

My parents met some of our relatives in Los Angeles and were creating a nice social circle. We had started the process of preparing and filing the paperwork to sponsor my sisters and their families to join us in the US. Every time we filed the papers, my sisters would apply, get denied and we would re-file and the entire process would take about a year. Giving up was not an option—resilience and persistence was the only path for us. My mother even wrote letters to President Reagan and Governor Deukmejian. It took seven years before my sisters and their families had permission to immigrate to the US. During those seven years, my mom visited them once and we were all overjoyed when they were finally allowed to join us.

My school was going OK during those years; the language was still a challenge. It was difficult for me to develop many friendships or have much of a social life as I was going to school full time and working. There was not much time left to socialize nor did I have the financial resources to spend on going out. I was struggling between my culture and the American cultures, wanting to assimilate yet wanting to keep some of my own cultural values and traditions. Coming from a family of engineers and being an immigrant, it was important to major in a subject that would result in a desirable and well-paying job. I started with a computer science major with the goal of being a programmer because programmers were in high demand, they got paid well and being in computer science did not require proficiency in English. However, after three years, I decided that I would not enjoy being a programmer, sitting in front of the computer all day, and changed my major to liberal studies. My parents were very disappointed and tried to talk me out of it, but I had made up my mind. I enjoyed the broader education rather than the specialized scope and I knew with liberal studies I had more options than just being a programmer.

Throughout college, I always worked about 30 hours a week, at a bank, at Levitz Furniture and at the counseling office at Glendale College. It took me five years to graduate since I had changed majors, although I did end up getting a minor in computer science as well because I already had so many classes toward that major.

Throughout the early '80s, I had been dating here and there, some longer relationships than others but I wasn't feeling the connection I was looking for with anyone. There was Ed, who was Armenian and went to USC studying engineering and seemed like a nice guy, but did not seem to have a backbone to stand up to his parents. His parents did not take my education very seriously and expected that once we got married, which we were not even discussing, I would be staying home and keeping myself busy like his mom did by raising children, being a "good" wife, socializing, shopping, making myself look good and whatever else she did. That choice certainly worked for some people, but it was not going to be my choice. Then there was John whom I met in college, an engineering major and he was a very nice guy, a gentleman, treated me with respect but we didn't really have any common interests. Then there was Nick who was a Levitz customer; he had been stationed in Germany for a while and now he was an electrical engineer. He was also nice and very handsome, but again, not a very interesting person. I was realizing that although many of the guys I was meeting were nice, educated and polite, none of them had a wide range of interests, had read any classical literature, or knew anything about art, poetry or classical music, nor did they have the wanderlust of wanting to experience life's many pleasures or travel. Then I met Richard at Levitz.

While I was still in college, I had gone to Levitz with my friend who was applying for a job and she convinced me to apply as well.

Although I already had a job, she thought it would be fun to work there together. I applied not even thinking I would get the job. I was surprised when they called me to go in for an interview. The supervisor who was supposed to interview me was out sick that day and the operations manager, who would have been the next person to interview me, was on vacation, so I ended up interviewing with Richard. Richard was very charming with a big smile and right away he detected my accent and asked me where I was from. I told him I was Armenian from the Soviet Union and he said that he was Polish, but was born and raised in Germany and moved to the US with his parents as a teenager. We felt an instant connection. We talked about our countries, cultures, our parents, and families and had a very enjoyable conversation learning about each other. I waited for him to ask me questions regarding the job but pretty soon, we had used up all the time and he had a meeting to go to so he told me that someone would be in touch with me. I thought to myself that this had been a waste of time, although I had enjoyed the conversation.

A few days later, I got an offer from them and shortly after I started work. It was close to school and home, so it was convenient. They had many young part-timers like me who also went to school so it was fun working there. We had company picnics and Christmas parties, we often went out dancing after work, and there was good camaraderie. We treated each other like family. Whenever Richard and I saw each other, we would engage in lengthy conversations and we quickly realized that we had many interests in common. He also went to the same gym I did and back in the '80s when aerobics classes were popular, he was often in the same class as me, wearing dolphin shorts and t-shirt. Most men did weights and very few were in the actual aerobics class. Richard was one of them, wearing the same white Reebok shoes as me. I also realized at Christmas parties or when we all went dancing that he not only loved dancing as much as I did, but he was a very good dancer, in many styles and enjoyed having fun. I did not know any men besides my father and Alex who were good at ballroom dancing. Most people couldn't even keep up with him when they danced with him. I guess with all that aerobic exercise, he was in great shape. Pretty soon he got comfortable enough where he would ask me about my dates or give me unsolicited advice and often joke with me. One day, a few days before my birthday, he heard my friends and I talking about going out to celebrate and later that day he said, "We should go out to celebrate your birthday. Are you available Friday evening?"

I hesitated because I wasn't sure if this was a date or a friendly invitation. "What did you have in mind?"

"We could go out to dinner or we could just get a bottle of wine, some cheese and croissants, take a blanket and go to the beach."

I laughed and didn't think he was really serious about the beach option. I asked him what time and where we should meet and, once we had that settled, I walked away. He knew I was dating Nick at that time, so I didn't think this was a date invitation. I also knew that we really enjoyed our conversations, but it was hard to have any lengthy conversations at work because we were both very busy.

Friday arrived and I was wearing a summer dress for the warm May weather and heels thinking we were going to dinner and when I arrived, he got out of his car to greet me and he was wearing shorts, a t-shirt and flip flops. I realized that we had a huge misunderstanding and that there was no way we were going to dinner so we both laughed and decided that we could just go to the beach and I could take my shoes off. We went in his car. He had prepared a picnic basket and brought a blanket, and we decided to go to Point Dume. It was still light out, but the sun was getting lower and the air was warm and pleasant, even though it was May. We set up for our picnic, enjoyed our bottle of chardonnay along with the cheese, croissants, grapes, and some chocolate. He also brought a tape player to listen to music too. We had similar taste in music and he enjoyed French, Italian and Spanish music, rock and classical music, as much as I did. That particular evening, we were listening to French accordion music by Enrique Macias. Over the years, I also learned to appreciate older music from the '50s and '60s, by listening to oldies when I was with Richard although some of it was familiar to me having been exposed to it when I was very young with my parents.

That afternoon at the beach, the conversation flowed and it felt like we had known each other forever. We talked about our childhoods, about music, books, art and what we like to do during our free time and we realized how much we both loved the outdoors, dancing and traveling. The sun started to set and it was beautiful at the beach. It also got a little colder. I didn't know if it was the wine or if we just had this amazing chemistry, but it felt really comfortable being with him. He put his arm around me and covered me with the blanket to keep me warm and soon it led to a kiss and another... When we were leaving, he said, "Listen, I really enjoyed being with you. I can't remember the last time I felt this way. Can I see you again?"

I said, "I had a really great time but I don't want to complicate things. I think I need to decide if I want to continue seeing Nick before I start anything with you."

"I understand, you just let me know. I would really love to see you again."

As I drove home after he dropped me off at my car, I felt very confused and torn. Could this be love again? I had a boyfriend, Richard and I worked at the same place, he was seventeen years older than me and had a child; yet at the same time, I hadn't felt this way with any of the guys I had dated since Alex. I couldn't even imagine he could be the right person for me, but at the same time, it felt so right. So many thoughts were going through my mind. I was not sure what I was going to do. I was thinking I made a mistake accepting his invitation and still, I was glad I had. I needed to sleep on it and really think this through. Part of me just did not want to see him again and part of me craved to see him again and soon. I did not sleep well that night.

The next morning, I was even more confused. My head told me to forget about our beach date, but my heart told me that I wanted to spend more time with him. What would I tell my parents? After all, he was not Armenian, he was much older than me, he was separated, he had a child; all things that would have been unacceptable by the Armenian community. Then there was Nick. I needed to take my time to really think this through. I also knew I would see Richard at work, and it would be awkward. A couple of days later, when I went out to dinner with Nick, all I could do was think about Richard. It made me realize that I did not have much in common with Nick and did not really enjoy spending time with him. Even though he was good looking guy, had a good job, was very nice to me, it was not enough, there was something missing—a connection that was so important to me—and the chemistry just was not there. Being with Nick that evening made me realize that

I could not be with him, knowing that there was someone like Richard out there. I thought, *What if I break up with him and then realize I made a mistake?* I thought I was being impulsive, it was just one evening with Richard, and I was just infatuated. First, I decided I should go out with Richard one more time, before I decided to break up with Nick, but then I realized that would not be fair to Nick. I had no connection with Nick, and it did not make sense to continue regardless of what happened with Richard. I ended my relationship with Nick and it actually felt OK.

The next few times I saw Richard at work, it was just in passing. I felt the tension and I wasn't sure if I should say anything and I could tell that maybe he wanted to but he didn't either. A few weeks later we had a company picnic, with food and games and lots of fun activities. Richard came up to me and asked me why I hadn't brought Nick to the picnic. That's when I told him I had broken up with Nick and although he said he was sorry, he had a little smile that he tried very hard not to show. We couldn't really talk too much about it at that moment or bring up anything personal as there were a lot of people around us and it was not the right setting for that conversation. A few hours later, as I walked to my car to go home, he said he would help me carry my chair and some other things and as we approached my car, he said, "Does that mean you will see me again?"

"Maybe we can go for a hike or something like that."

He smiled and asked, "How about next Friday? I can look up a few places and make suggestions."

"OK, but not too far. I have another commitment in the evening."

"OK."

I got in my car and left, wondering if I was making a good decision. Although I was apprehensive about it, part of me was very excited and felt the butterflies of anticipation. I tried to justify to myself that it wasn't like I was getting married to the guy. There was nothing wrong in spending time with someone I enjoyed being with. I decided not to worry about the future or about telling my parents about him as of yet. By the time I got home, I had convinced myself that this was not a bad decision and started thinking about the upcoming hike. I looked forward to spending more time with Richard.

The Era of Richard

Richard and I got to spend more and more time together. We went ballroom dancing at Alpine Village, swing dancing at the Derby and danced to Motown music at Crush Bar. We often had picnics at the park, went to the Hollywood Bowl or Dorothy Chandler for classical music, visited the various art exhibits in LA, spent time at the beach, and went to the library or bookstores to find some good reads. We loved hiking and biking locally, camping and backpacking in Yosemite, King National Park and many other places including climbing Mt. Whitney. In the winter, we went skiing either locally to Big Bear, or to Mammoth, to Lake Tahoe, Mt. Bachelor in Oregon, Vail and Beaver Creek in Colorado, Brian Head in Utah, and Taos New Mexico.

The more time we spent together and the better we got to know each other, the more we wanted to be together. When I shared with him my decision to change majors, he was very supportive and encouraged me to follow my heart. He had studied to be an engineer and worked as an engineer for a little while but got into retail business because he felt that engineering was not the right profession for him and was not fulfilling. He regretted that he hadn't made the change while still in school like I did. He accepted me completely without judgment and without any desire to change anything about me. With Richard, I felt like I had never felt before with anyone since I had been in the US. We spent hours just reading poetry or listening to songs that reflected our love, our circumstances, and our feelings for each other. We constantly planned our next opportunity to be together. Back then, there were no cell phones and with our schedules between my school and both of our jobs, it was hard to always carve out the time. He often left me love notes on my car windshield, and I left him notes in my brown paper lunch bag in the refrigerator at work for him to get.

We were in a relationship but there was a hesitation and worry that was always in the back of my mind. I wasn't sure if what I was feeling was real. It felt too good to be true. I constantly worried where all this was going to lead us. He was separated but not divorced yet, and even if that became a non-issue, there was still the age difference, a child in the equation and the fact that he was a non-Armenian. I didn't know how my parents would react.

When I had gone to Hawaii with my parents one summer and upon our return home, there was a yellow ribbon tied around our front tree. Neither my parents nor I knew what that was for or who had tied it. The next day Richard had asked me if I noticed the yellow ribbon on the tree and I said yes and asked him what it was for and he said he wanted me to know how much he missed me the minute I got home and that was one way he could think of doing it. I thought that was so romantic. I felt so alive when I was with him yet I was in despair when we were apart. It felt like the forbidden love but felt so right at the same time. I couldn't really share my feelings with others because my parents didn't know about him and I wasn't sure if this was a temporary situation or true love that would last.

Over the months, thoughts of ending the relationship would cross my mind. I was not sure if my family would accept my relationship. I did not know anyone in my circle of Armenian friends and family who had married a non-Armenian or someone who was divorced or someone who had a child. In addition, I was not sure if this relationship would last. Was he just another guy going through a mid-life crisis and had found a younger girlfriend? I also worried that people would judge me and I was insecure about that. Even with all those concerns and mixed emotions, I couldn't end the relationship. Being with him was like a drug that I could not give up. He understood me so well and he knew what my needs were, what made me smile, what my boundaries were and what made me excited and vulnerable.

He had an amazing capacity to accept and love people as they came. He lived his life to the fullest and didn't worry much about anything, didn't judge himself for his mistakes or others for their imperfections. He lived with no regrets. He was a positive influence on me in terms of having an open mind and open heart beyond my imagination or anyone's expectations. He made me feel enough and full—full of life, full of joy, full of hope, full of anticipation and full of lightness about life. It felt like when we were together, we were in a bubble, away from all our worries, all the world's problems, all our responsibilities and all the people that were in our lives.

When I graduated in 1986, I had several job opportunities from various sectors: CIA, retail, and the insurance industry. The one from the CIA sounded the most exciting. I had finished my third interview and I was sharing with my parents the potential opportunity with the CIA when they gave me a little reality check. They expressed their concern that if I accepted a job with the CIA,

I could be used for going back and forth to the Soviet Union and my sisters may never have the opportunity to come to the US. I don't know how true that was, but I could never put myself in that position where because of my career choice, my sisters were not able to move to the US. I loved my parents and my sisters too much to make that choice and I knew I would regret it the rest of my life. As my father had taught us, family always came first. I decided to take the position with Prudential Insurance as a Long-Term Disability Claim Examiner making $18,600 a year. My mother pointed out that had I chosen to be a programmer, I could be making $25,000 a year. I did not really care, because I was happy with my choice.

I continued working at Levitz Furniture for a while part time in addition to my full-time job because I wanted to save money to buy a brand new car. I would work at Prudential from 7:00 a.m. and 3:30 p.m., and then work at Levitz from 4:00 or 5:00 p.m. until 10:00 p.m. and on weekends, but I was happy and super excited when I had saved enough money and was able to buy my Toyota Celica. It was so nice to have a car that I did not constantly have to worry about breaking down. I was so proud of my car that I even stood next to it and took a picture that I sent to my sisters.

Reuniting With My Sisters – 1987

T he weeks and months flew by. I had left my second job at Levitz Furniture. When I started working at Prudential, my parents offered to make me 25% owner of the house they had purchased if I stayed home and made 25% of the payments. It seemed like it was a good arrangement. It helped them financially and I was building some equity and was able to pay for all my expenses. I had been working at Prudential for about a year when we were notified that my sisters had approval to immigrate to the US with their families. My parents and I were ecstatic. It was hard to believe that after so many years, they were finally going to join us. When we left them, my niece had been almost three years old and my nephew almost two. Now they were ten and nine years old. I could not wait to see them and spoil them. They had bought their tickets up to Washington, DC and we got them tickets from Washington, DC to Los Angeles. We decided that I would meet them in Washington DC and travel to Los Angeles with them. This was the first year that I had gotten a bonus at work and the timing was perfect. I used that money to buy red-eye tickets through Chicago to Washington, DC to meet my sisters and their families.

I got to Washington, DC early that morning and their flight was not coming until later in the afternoon. Although I was tired, since I had never been in Washington, DC, I decided to leave the airport and do some site-seeing instead of waiting at the airport. I was excited to see DC, even if it was just for few hours. After all, that's where the White House was, that's where the president lived and it was our nation's capital. It was an emotional moment for me as I had lived in the US for seven years by then and still had not seen our capital. I really enjoyed the visit and even walked the National Mall and got to see the White House, the Washington Monument and Lincoln Memorial.

I came back to the airport just in time to meet them as they were arriving. Seeing my sisters, their spouses and their children come through customs was one of the happiest moments in my life. I had missed them so much. It was hard to believe that they were finally here. I was a child when I had left them, and now I was an adult. I was anxious to get to know them and for them to get to know me now, in different stages in our lives. I almost felt that I could have a different relationship with them now than before. I could be closer to them because the age difference did not feel as wide as before. I was not a child any more and I really craved to have that sisterly closeness that I thought Arous and Annie had because they were so much closer in age. I loved my sisters, but I felt that between the age difference and the seven years we were apart and having lived in different countries, it was going to take some time before we felt the closeness that sisters should feel and be able to share our inner feelings and thoughts.

The first thing I did at the airport was take my niece and nephew to the candy store while we were waiting for the connecting flight to Los Angeles and asked them to pick whatever they wanted. Seeing the sparkle in their eyes made my heart smile. They probably had never seen so many different types of candies in one store and it took them a while to decide, and it was a pure pleasure for me.

Of course, when we got to Los Angeles, my parents were so happy and emotional, there were lots of tears and the welcome party was already planned for the coming weekend. We had relatives, coworkers, friends and neighbors invited to the party and they were all very happy for us. They all knew how important this was for us and how hard it had been to wait for so many years. We had the party in our backyard with lots of food, drinks, music and, of course, dancing. Now our family was complete again. My mom never ever wanted to talk about Armenia again or go back to visit.

At Prudential, I was the columnist for "Miss Manners" section of the Espresso newspaper we published monthly. When they heard that my sisters were arriving from Armenia, one of the writers wrote an article about them and it was published along with our picture from the Washington, DC airport when they had just arrived. So many people were excited and happy for us. Along with our relatives, friends and coworkers, even strangers that heard our story celebrated with us. Of course, Richard was thrilled for me as well.

I wanted so badly for him to meet my sisters, although I was not sure what their reaction would be, but my parents still did not know about him and I was hoping the day would come soon that I would finally have the courage to tell them about Richard.

My sisters' families lived with us for a while, until they got jobs. We had a three-bedroom house, so we made the dining room into another bedroom, my nephew slept in my parents' room on a cot, and my niece slept in my room. It was happy times, with all of us under one roof and there was lots of love and joy and sharing. After all, that's what family is all about.

One of my fondest memories was the first Christmas we celebrated together after my sisters joined us. In Armenia, Christmas was celebrated on January 6th according to the Julian calendar and it was strictly religious holiday. There were no gifts and we just had a simple meal of fish, rice and sautéed spinach with yogurt. New Year's Eve was celebrated with the Christmas tree, except we called it a holiday tree. That's when Santa Clause came at midnight of New Year's Eve and we called him Winter Grandpa, and children got one gift for the New Year and usually we had to sing or dance or recite a poem before Santa gave you the gift. When I was young, my parents would make me take a nap in the evening for a couple of hours so I could stay up until midnight to celebrate the New Year. One year my mom was Santa; and although she had a Santa costume on, she was not wearing gloves and I recognized her hands. I did not want to say anything because I still wanted to get my gift.

Starting January 1st and for the next few days, we visited relatives and they visited us to wish Happy New Year and it always involved a lot of food, drinking and dancing. I looked forward to sharing the new tradition with my niece and nephew. I slept in the living room Christmas Eve with them. We left milk and cookies for Santa, which was something new for them and seeing their bright and smiling eyes in the morning and knowing that they still believed in Santa made this one of the best Christmases ever. I enjoyed watching them open their presents and I don't even remember what presents they got, but seeing their excitement was something I will never forget.

Similar to my parents and I, my sisters and brothers-in-law were all enrolled in English as a second language classes when they first got to the US. My sister Annie went through a bookkeeping program and was able to get a bookkeeping job, my sister Arous went through a computer programming course and also was able to get a job, and both my brothers-in-law got jobs as well. Shortly after they started working, they got their own places and moved out but still lived very close to my parents and we got to see them and spend time with them frequently. My niece and nephew were enrolled in school and quickly adapted to the new school, new language and new environment. They were doing really great and I was enjoying getting to know them seven years later.

In the meantime, Richard and I continued our relationship but still not many people knew about it. My parents had not met him and of course, I didn't know how I could tell my sisters yet. During our relationship, on a few occasions, I took a break with the attempt to test the relationship or question my feelings and every time, I longed to be back with him. A couple of times, I even went out on dates with other guys, but my heart was not in it. I loved Richard and I felt my best when I was with him. He was patient with me and understood that I needed to be sure before I introduced him to my parents and brought any unnecessary heartache or concerns to them.

My mom suspected that I was seeing someone and sometimes she would ask me questions when I went out or went away for few days but I had not had the courage to tell her. Once my sisters were here, she made comments to them about me and said she suspected that I was dating someone. Perhaps she was hoping that I would say something to them or they could find out by asking me questions. At times, I wished I could share my secret with them, but I was hesitant, I was still working on developing a closer relationship with them. Even though our age differences did not seem as large, we were still in different places in our lives and had different priorities and it was hard to overcome that barrier and only time would allow us to get to that next level of intimate closeness.

I knew I was not going to give up Richard, as I loved him so much. However, I also could not continue living with this secret; it was emotionally draining. I read a "Dear Abby" column where a woman from Middle East living in the US with her family was dating an American man. Her parents told her that she couldn't date a foreigner and if she continued, they would disown her. She pointed out that, in fact, she was the foreigner, not the man she was dating and if anyone, it should be his parents who should feel that way. That struck a chord with me and I knew I had to be true to my parents and myself. I was not the only daughter that my parents had in the US any longer and if they decided to disown me because of this, it would be hurtful and be a shame, but at least they had two other daughters and I hoped that over time they would accept it. I also felt that perhaps I could get the support of my sisters and my mom's curiosity would be finally satisfied. So I finally had the courage to tell my parents.

Their reaction was not as bad as I anticipated. Once I told them all the things about Richard that I thought would concern them, they had to take the time to let it all sink in. Finally, the day came when Richard came to meet my family. Of course, my mom had prepared dinner, we had drinks and the conversation went well but I think my dad was still not completely comfortable with the idea. He drank a lot and this was the first time in my life that I ever felt my dad drank too much and it showed. He eventually had to go lie down in the bedroom because he didn't feel well. However, overall, the meeting went better than I'd expected, and the first impressions were positive. My family came to love Richard over time and, at times, I wonder why I was so apprehensive about it but knowing how they felt about him, and most importantly, how I felt with him, I knew I had made the right choice.

Memorable Greek Festival

Richard and I were at the Greek Festival in May of 1990. We loved the food, the music and the dancing and we had gone several times before. As usual, we danced with many other people in a big circle to Greek music, and the next thing I knew, he was down on his knee telling me something. I thought it was just another Greek dance move and since the music was so loud, I couldn't really hear what he was saying. I kept asking, "What? What?" Until one of the other dancers who could apparently hear him better than me said, "He is proposing to you." First, I thought it was a joke. Here, in front of all these people? Then I heard him say it again.

"Arminé, you are my best friend and love of my life. Will you marry me?"

I started laughing nervously and didn't quite know what to do or say, especially in front of all those people. One of the dancers then said, "Say yes."

I did say yes, and we kissed, continued dancing and celebrating. What I loved about it was that it felt spontaneous, not staged and he didn't even have a ring, which was the least important thing to me. I was overwhelmed by the moment, surprised it happened so quickly after he had met my family but I felt comfortable with the idea since we had been together for several years already, although I always thought I didn't want to get married until I was 30.

We started planning for a wedding shortly. We did not see any reason to wait since we had been together for so long. At that time, I had met Michael, Richard's son, only a few times as his father's friend and had not spent much time with him. It was important to get to know him a little better and spend more time with him so we started going to museums with him, or swimming in the pool at Richard's apartment, going to the library or out to eat. I also often went to his baseball, basketball or soccer games and got to meet his mom as well and we had a cordial relationship. He was shy but did not resist meeting me and we got along fine. The more time we spent together, the more comfortable he got.

With the wedding planning, once again we had to consider cultural differences and make some compromises. Armenians usually have a very traditional church wedding and a very large reception. I always loved the outdoor weddings because I thought they were more beautiful and it resonated more with our love for the outdoors and I liked small weddings. It was difficult to find an Armenian priest who would perform a wedding outside the church, but my parents wanted a priest that could at least say a few things in Armenian. We finally found one who could perform the ceremony outside the church in English but also say a few things in Armenian. When we interviewed him, we found out that he had also married Hugh Hefner and Kimberley Conrad and ironically, our son and his son Cooper Hefner were in the same summer camp years later.

At the same time, we looked to buy a house where we would live together. We had looked at some homes in the San Fernando

Valley but hadn't found anything we liked in our price range. One day, when Richard was on a business trip in Florida, I saw advertising for new homes in Oak Park. I didn't even know where Oak Park was but looking it up on the map, it did not seem too far. I decided to go for the opening day where they were going to release the first phase just to check it out. Once I got there, I noticed that there were a lot of people. They had the model homes you could look at and if you were interested, you could put your name down for the first phase. Since there were more people interested than homes available, they decided to use a lottery system. With my luck, they called my name and fortunately I had a checkbook with me and was able to give them a $5,000 deposit and got one of the homes, which was still being built.

Later that day, when Richard called, I told him what had happened, and I was nervous about his reaction as he hadn't even seen the home and he, like me, didn't know where Oak Park was. I was pleasantly surprised that he was OK with it and said, "If you like it and you think we can afford it, then I am fine with it." When he got back, we went there so he could see the model home and the actual lot where our home was going to be built and he was very happy with it. We considered ourselves fortunate that they had called my name through the lottery system. We got married in September of 1990. We had a morning wedding by the beautiful waterfalls in Calabasas followed by a lunch reception and lots of dancing. We had written our simple vows and our priest said as he concluded the ceremony, "Remember, the grass is not green on the other side, the grass is green where you water it." I have written that in many wedding cards throughout the years.

My niece and my nephew were in the wedding as junior bridesmaid and groomsman, Richard's brother John was the best man, my friend Jackie was the maid of honor, my stepson Michael was the ring bearer and we had two flower girls, Maggie and Lilit. I couldn't be happier to have found love and a best friend to be my life partner. We left for our honeymoon to the Greek Islands the next day. Although we had been away together before, our honeymoon was truly an amazing experience for us.

He had given up his apartment before we left and our house was not ready yet when we returned so we lived with my parents for a couple of week and then were able to move to our new house together. This was the first time we were going to live together after so many years of being together and certainly vacations had been great but living together was going to be different. I was also a parent now and I was not sure how Michael and I would get along. Richard had 50% custody of Michael so he was with us 50% of the time. It did not seem too difficult to adjust to it. Richard had an amicable relationship with his ex-wife and his ex-in-laws. Michael's mom often traveled for work and his grandparents on his mom's side were always willing to help out with Michael's school pick up and drop off and all his sports activities. Michael was eight when we got married and I had only gotten to know him a little better a few months before we got married. Although he was reserved and did not always show much emotion, over time he slowly warmed up to my family and me. It helped that I had a niece and nephew close to his age and Richard often took them camping and on weekend activities. Michael had an amazing memory, he was very smart and an easygoing child who loved sports and video games. Our living room and dining area was one large room and was empty for a long time, so we used to play football with Michael in that room.

When we first lived together, I did not know how to cook, so Richard did a lot of the cooking and he was a good cook. After seeing how much he enjoyed cooking with a glass of wine in the evenings, I decided I wanted to learn how to cook and we often cooked together which we both enjoyed. Michael was a picky eater and we had to prepare separate meals for him. We enjoyed living together, getting into our routines, slowly decorating our home, doing the landscaping. It felt easy to adjust to living together and we realized that we were similar in many ways, but not in every way. Richard was more relaxed and easy-going and I was more impatient and more of a taskmaster. He was a procrastinator and I wanted to get things done right away. We were both giving and helpful so we did not feel any pressure or challenges in terms of getting household chores done, we both stepped in and did what needed to be done without any thoughts about the traditional roles of men and women and it worked well for us. There was definitely unity and harmony with occasional disagreements and mostly it was me who was more particular and less flexible.

Welcoming Kyle into Our Life

S hortly after we got married, I got pregnant Thanksgiving weekend and Richard made a surprise announcement to my family on Christmas Eve by gifting my parents a baby bootie. Of course, my family was overjoyed and there was yet another reason for celebration. I had a comfortable and healthy pregnancy and felt strong through the end. Richard packed granola and yogurt for me for breakfast every day and carrots and fruits for afternoon snack and since he was a big fan of health food stores, I got the freshest of produce. I learned from him about vitamins and minerals and what to look for when reading the ingredients of anything I bought and it definitely stayed with me to this day. He played classical music and put the little speaker on my belly for the baby to hear and we often got a reaction from the baby or we thought we did. Not much slowed me down and I continued with all my regular activities, including my workouts and as it started getting hotter in the summer, I was swimming every day. We did not want to find out what we were having, just having a healthy baby was what we wished for, although later he told me he was secretly wishing for a girl for me as he thought all women love having daughters.

I decided to work through the end since I felt so well. I started my maternity leave on a Monday and Richard left for a business trip to Las Vegas on Wednesday and returned Friday. I thought I had another week before the baby was born. On Thursday, I felt some contractions and had a doctor's appointment. After examining me, my doctor told me that I was going to have the baby that day and needed to go to the hospital. I came home, called Richard and told him I was having the baby, got my bag and drove myself to the hospital even though he told me to call my parents to take me. He took the next flight and was at the hospital a few hours later. Soon my entire family was there in the waiting room. It was August, during the summer break from school and my sister Annie had been at Raging Waters Water Park with my niece, nephew and stepson that day and they all came straight to the hospital to meet the new baby. My labor was prolonged and my niece, my nephew and Michael were very tired after being in the water park most of the day and had fallen asleep in the waiting room.

It was past midnight. The current event at that time was the "perestroika" in Russia and my doctor and Richard were talking about that. At some point, I got annoyed with it and pointed out that I was in labor and having a baby and needed their attention on me. They were just joking around and trying to keep my mind away from the pain. My doctor had even canceled his dinner plans with his wife to be there with me.

Finally, Kyle was born at 2:17 a.m. on Friday, August 16. He was 8.5 pounds and 21 inches, healthy with a loud scream. His birth was one of the most joyous moments in my life, a moment that is hard to anticipate or describe but I instantly fell in love with my baby. I held him and never ever wanted to put him down. It felt like a miracle, a deep joyous feeling that one can only experience but would be difficult to describe. After Richard held him too, my doctor invited my mom into the labor and delivery room and whoever else in my family that wanted to come meet him and hold him. At first my mom was hesitant because you could never do that in Armenia, but then she was so excited to be able to hold the baby just after he was born. Kyle had a smile on his face even at his first few moments of life. I knew at that moment that he was going to be a happy person the rest of his life.

A New Stage in Our Life

I took ten weeks off after Kyle was born before I went back to work. I was exploring childcare options and was ready to hire someone to come to the house but my parents surprised me with their decision to retire and the timing was perfect. I was still working at Prudential but I had changed departments and gotten promoted and I was ready to go back to work. My parents watched Kyle four days a week. Richard was off on Fridays and Saturdays, so he was with Kyle on Fridays and we had family time on Saturdays, as that was the only day we both had off. I was home with Kyle on Sundays. Kyle grew up a happy baby, infinitely curious and on the move non-stop. He was such a joy to be around. When he started to crawl at seven months, sometimes he crawled backwards. He started walking at ten months. Once he was on the move, it was hard to keep up with him. He started pre-school when he was two, which was an on-site daycare at my job, making it very convenient. He adjusted well and was probably one of the very few kids who did not nap, although he slept really well at night from when I went back to work and anytime he was tired. Regardless of where we were, or how noisy it was, he could fall asleep. He was a spirited child and when he was awake, he was always on the go, always up for an outing. He had a hunger for learning and experiencing things. He loved people and playing with other kids and had no issues spending the night with his grandparents or aunts. Things were going well for me at work. I rotated through different assignments and advanced. Richard still loved being a store manager at Levitz Furniture.

In January of 1994 Kyle was almost two and a half years old when we had the Northridge earthquake. The earthquake was about 4:30 in the morning and Kyle's bedroom was on the other side of the house. He didn't wake up from it by himself and both Richard and I woke up from the shaking and once we realized how strong it was, we ran toward his room to get him. Richard grabbed him from his bed and ran downstairs and I followed him. Kyle woke up from all the commotion. He felt the panic in us and began to cry.

Once we were downstairs, Richard handed Kyle to me and pulled his car out of the garage just in case there was an aftershock and something happened which resulted in not being able to open the garage door. He ran to a couple of the neighbors and encouraged them to do the same. As he did that, he got a call from Levitz's emergency line telling him about the extensive damage. Since he was the store manager, he had to go to work and meet the emergency assessment team. Once he made sure we were OK, he left. After he was gone, I also got a call from work telling me that it was not safe to go to work until they assessed the damage and frankly I did not want to leave Kyle to go to work. Kyle was shaken up over the earthquake and for a while, whenever he saw something broken, he said, "The earthquake did it." We had some broken things but my parents lived closer to the epicenter and had more damage. Thankfully, it wasn't major.

Kyle did not want to sleep in his bed for a while after that and it took us a while to retrain him to sleep in his bed. The biggest impact for us was that Levitz Furniture, which was in Northridge at the epicenter of the earthquake, had extensive damaged and had to be demolished and rebuilt. This meant Richard had no workplace.

The year and four months it took to rebuild the store were difficult times for us. In the beginning, Richard was busy getting everything organized and coordinating to have the work started. Thankfully, he was a structural engineer by education and had some past experience. That helped influence the architects in creating a modern design. Then he was sent to Chicago for few months to help with the new store they had opened up. Although I visited him once for a long weekend for our anniversary, it was hard when he was away. When he returned, he would drive to the Huntington Beach store in Orange County, spending three to four hours every day on the road. The long days were very tiring and although he never complained, I could see it on him. It took a toll on me as well because I was essentially a single parent, dropping Kyle off, picking him up, feeding him and doing what was needed to keep things going. We had to rely on Michael's grandparents for help with Michael. We wanted him to go to school where we lived as we had very good public schools and it made things easier, but his mom felt strongly about sending him to private school. His school was not close to us or to his mom, but we were thankful that his grandparents were retired and could help both his mom and us with school and sports activities.

Finally, the store re-opened in May of 1995 and life got back to normal for us. In the same year, I decided I wanted to go back to school to get my MBA. I started an evening program at

Pepperdine University while still working full time. I completed the program in three years. I still worked for Prudential and they paid 90% of my tuition, which was a gift, as we could not afford to pay for it given our other priorities. I was very thankful for Richard and his support and I knew I couldn't have done it without his love and support. He was so proud of me and was very excited for me when I completed the program. After graduation, we celebrated by having dinner in Malibu with my family. He always praised me to others, with or without my presence, and expressed his appreciation which made me feel valued and loved. I felt so fortunate to be married to someone like him, and I was grateful to have him as my husband and father of my son. He was a kind, loving, caring man who brought a smile to everyone's face and warmed everyone's heart. Richard always believed that if you didn't have anything nice to say, then it was not worth saying anything at all, and he lived by that.

Reconnecting with Alex

O ne day in the summer of 1994, I was at my parents' house with Kyle and they had a friend visiting from Armenia. They had two daughters close to my age and we used to have picnics with their family in the summer and ski in the winter. As I reminisced with my mom's friend and asked her about her daughters, she mentioned that they were neighbors with Alex's parents. I had never even realized she knew Alex. I was surprised to hear that and of course was very curious to hear about how Alex and his family were doing. She told me that Alex had gotten married and was living in Tambov, Russia and she shared a little bit about how his family was doing. It was nice to get an update about them. When she was getting ready to leave, I asked her if she would take a letter to Alex for me and give it to his parents to send it to Alex and she agreed. I wrote to Alex about my life, that I had gotten married and had a son, about our classmates who lived in Los Angeles, and I sent him a picture of Kyle. I also told him that a long time had passed, and I hoped he had forgiven me and that I would love to hear about his life and his family and included my address and phone number.

I did not hear anything back for a long time. I thought he was still mad at me and had no interest in reconnecting. Then, one day in 1997, I got a letter from him. He apologized that it had taken him such a long time to respond and explained what had happened. Although his parents had gotten my letter, they did not mail it to Alex because they were worried that it would make his wife jealous because Alex often spoke about me. They decided to give it to him in person when he visited them. Alex did not visit for a couple of years and when he finally went to Armenia in 1997 for his mother's funeral, that's when he got my letter. His sister had found the letter and gave it to him at that time. He said he was happy to hear from me and wrote about his family, about his children, about his work and life in Tambov and also indicated that he was still doing woodcarving and would like to send one of his carvings to me as a gift. He included his address and phone number.

A few months later, I got a beautifully carved wood face with a small note. I wrote him back thanking him for the gift and indicated that I wanted to send some gifts for his children, which I did a few months later. He wrote me back thanking me for it and included a poem he had written for me years back. It was a beautiful poem and reminded me of how poetic and romantic his soul was. We exchanged a few more letters through 1997 and 1998 and then he wrote to me indicating that he was not going to continue corresponding with me because it was bringing many memories back and his heart was aching and it was better to leave things buried as they had been for all those years. I did not write back to him.

On my birthday in 1999, he surprised me by calling me and wishing me a happy birthday, asking if I was upset with him because he did not want to continue writing and indicating that he missed our friendship and wanted to keep in touch. I thanked him for remembering my birthday, told him I was not upset, and I would love to keep in touch. We talked about his father-in-law living in the US and his wife wanting to come visit and I told him that if they came to California, I would love to meet his wife and have him meet my family. He said he had no desire to come to the US and the conversation ended shortly. In the next few years, he called me a handful of times, and I could tell from his voice he really enjoyed our conversations and hearing about Kyle and sharing with me about his children. It always felt as though there was more he wanted to say, but he was holding back.

Happy Years after the Earthquake

Richard and I enjoyed our life together, and appreciated that we were back to normalcy after his store was rebuilt and I had finished my MBA program. Kyle grew up and became even more energetic, curious and loveable. He enjoyed our many family vacations through the US, Hawaii, Canada, Mexico and was a great traveler, taking it all in. Michael was with us on vacations too and at times, I wished he made more effort to bond with his little brother, but I did not sense he was interested. He often appeared distant and although we never had any challenges in our relationship, I always felt that he resented his parents' divorced and his father having a new family, although we made every effort to make sure he felt part of the new family. I had my own insecurities about it, naturally, but Richard always reassured me, which helped a lot.

Richard and I had talked about going to Europe and we were waiting for Kyle to be a little older to do that. Richard had been promoted to a Market Manager, which meant that he was overseeing several Levitz stores throughout Southern California with long travel times and his schedule was more unpredictable and the new management demanded more of his time. I also accepted a new position with Health Net, which was a promotion for me with opportunity to grow, with more responsibilities and a less flexible schedule. Between the two of us, it was more difficult to coordinate pick-ups and drop-offs, doctor and dentist appointments and after school activities. We talked about hiring help now that I was making more money and we did for a short time, but then we discussed buying a bigger house so my parents could come live with us. We thought that would help us with Kyle's activities, and it would help my parents as they were getting older, living on limited income and they had enjoyed traveling with us but financially it was becoming more difficult. Living with us would allow them to enjoy their later years, going on more trips and doing things they couldn't otherwise afford.

The timing also felt right as Michael was graduating from an all-boys Catholic high school and was planning to go to Penn State for college. Once again, I felt that Michael was not very interested in staying close to us, wanted to be away from family and did not care to be close to his brother and truly be a big brother to Kyle. After all, they only had each other, and I very much wanted them to grow up to be close and be in each other's lives. Even though he had been part of my family and had been exposed to the warm, caring, giving family culture we promoted, it was hard to get him to express his emotions or express any warmth or affection toward his father, Kyle or me. I never lost my hope though and loved him and thought that one day he would mature and realize the importance of family and the importance of staying close.

We discussed the idea with my parents, and they liked it and were actually excited to live with us, spend more time with Kyle, take him to soccer practice or pick him up from school and have that family closeness. How fortunate for Kyle that he would have his grandparents so involved in his life. That wasn't something most kids in the US had the opportunity to have and for us, it was a privilege and a pleasure to continue with the traditions we grew up with.

We started looking for a new house and initially it was hard to find a house that had two large bedrooms, as we wanted my parents to have a good size bedroom as well. After some time though, we were able to find one being built and we were able to have second master bedroom for my parents and a separate sitting area for them. My parents and Richard and I sold our existing homes and moved into the new house in October of 2000. Things were going well; we adjusted to living together and there was a lot less pressure for me and Richard in regards to having to take time off from work to manage Kyle's many activities.

Although the house was brand new, we still had to furnish it, hardscape and landscape the backyard, add window coverings and other things that new houses need. We knew we would be settled in by spring of 2001 and we could go on our trip to Europe that summer. We were very happy with how all the improvements came out and we even had a friend's 40th surprise birthday party at our house in May prior to going on our trip. Kyle was almost ten in June of 2001 when we went on our three-week trip to Europe. My parents were excited to join us on our trip as they had done on many other trips to Canada, Mexico, Hawaii and other parts of the US.

We flew to London and after spending a few days there, we took the hovercraft across the channel to Calais and rented a car. We drove throughout Europe and it was an excellent way to see things that you normally would not get a chance to see. Richard was very excited to show Kyle his neighborhood, his apartment, and the school he had attended in Munich, Germany. It was one of many memorable trips we had but this one was particularly special because Kyle got to see where his father grew up. When we were in Venice, Richard took a picture of Kyle with the pigeons in St. Mark Square, which looked identical to a picture that Richard had of himself in Venice when he was in his early twenties. It was an amazing experience and having my parents there and seeing them enjoying the trip and being there with us was very special.

Traveling and seeing through children's eyes adds its own special perspective and it was so gratifying to see how Kyle was tirelessly keeping up with all of us and taking in all that we did there. But then again, who wouldn't enjoy being around someone like Richard, with his positive outlook, high energy and a fun personality? And let's not forget my organizational skills. I had an entire spreadsheet for every city we were going to visit, every hotel, and every activity but left some room for spontaneous activities. I knew one day I wanted to take Richard and Kyle to Yerevan, Armenia so they could see where I grew up. I couldn't wait to do that.

Our Life Changed Forever
– December 11, 2001

After we came back from Europe, we went back to our routines with work, school, sports and family events and all was going well, although Richard's schedule really concerned me. First, we had 9/11, which was not anything we ever expected to experience in our lifetime in this country. I was driving to work when Richard called me to tell me about it. It was almost surreal and made me feel like I did not want to go to work; I wanted to go back home to be with my family. It was tragic and heartbreaking and there was heaviness about it but somehow, we continued with our routine, somewhat less affected than people who lived in New York. But the year was not over yet, and we were still mourning with the families who lost someone in the attack.

A couple of weeks before Christmas, we had completed our Christmas decorations the weekend before, the tree and lights were up, and the holidays were just around the corner. On Saturday evening, we got together with some of our Oak Park friends and their families and Sunday my family had come over for dinner, before the busy holiday season.

On Mondays Richard worked late and when he got home, I was watching *Ally McBeal* and it was the episode "Nine One One." It was right before Christmas and Ally was trying to convince a reverend's son (played by Josh Groban)—who had just lost his mother and as a result had lost his faith in God, and did not want to sing in church any longer—that his mother was still here and he will sing again. He was able to believe in God again and the first song he sang at church was "To Where You Are." The lyrics gutted me and I thought to myself that if anything ever happened to Richard, that's exactly how I would feel and I could not imagine the pain he and his father felt for their loss. When Richard walked in, I had tears in my eyes and he asked me if I was OK and I told him what had happened in that episode and about the song and how beautiful it was and how I could never imagine losing him. He hugged me, kissed me and told me that I did not need to worry about that; nothing was going to happen to him.

It was Tuesday, December 11, 2001 when I started my day, thinking it was another ordinary day. As I got ready that morning, I thought about my "to do" list for the upcoming Saturday, for the holiday party we were going to host with my work friends. Richard had gone running that morning with our dog Peaches, Kyle was getting ready for school and I was getting ready for work. I was going to work from our Woodland Hills office that day instead of my main office in Ventura because I was going to attend some meetings there. My plan was to go buy the karaoke machine after work, an early Christmas present for Richard, so we could use it during our party.

My morning at work was pretty uneventful. I had lunch with a friend who knew a lot about karaoke machines and I wanted to get his recommendations and my afternoon was going to be in meetings with my boss and others. We talked about different songs and what songs were good for karaoke singing; we also talked about different music we listened to when we were young and what bands we liked. We talk about Pink Floyd and how "Wish You Were Here" was always one of my favorite songs and how much I loved the words.

I also told him that I was excited about the karaoke machine and in general was in good spirits with the holidays coming up. I looked forward to taking some time off to be with family. I hoped that Richard could take a day or two off to just rest. He had been working long hours and six days a week for over a year now, since he had become a market manager. Even when he was home in the evenings or we were out somewhere, he would get urgent calls and he had to always take the calls. I could see the stress on his face, even though he never complained. This year was the first time he had missed trick-or-treating for Halloween and hadn't been able to take any days off during Thanksgiving weekend except Thanksgiving Day itself. Sensing the pressure he was under, I had encouraged him to also go for a physical to make sure everything was OK. A few times when he had come back from running, I had noticed the marks on his back from lying down on the picnic table in the park to do sit ups and it did not look right to me. Later I learned that when you take baby aspirin, which thins your blood, bruises show easily.

We had had a long discussion about his new role a week before and I told him the higher salary was not worth it as it was impacting his health. I encouraged him to step down to a store manager. It was not an easy decision for him as he did not want to let down his leadership team and he was worried how the leadership team would view it. Several people had lost their jobs with the leadership changes and he was concerned that this may result in him losing his job too. I told him that even if he did, we would be OK, and he could get another job. His health was more important, and I did not care about the money. He finally agreed that he would have that conversation with his boss and ask to step down to being a store manager again after the holidays, once things slowed down a little.

During my meetings in the early afternoon, my cell phone rang. I just ignored it because I didn't recognize the number, but then it rang again a few more times from the same number. I put it on vibrate and just thought they were probably trying to sell me something. After about five to ten minutes, while I was still in the meeting, my phone vibrated and it was my home number. I ignored it again, thinking Kyle was home by now from school and probably wanted to ask me something; he could leave me a message and I would call him back after the meeting.

Then it kept vibrating a few more times from my home number. By this time, my boss was very irritated that my phone kept vibrating and said, "Can you just shut your phone off?" in a tone that made me feel really guilty for disrupting the meeting and embarrassed in front of others. As I turned it off, something did not feel right in my gut. Kyle rarely called me at work and certainly not repeatedly. It felt like someone was really trying to get a hold of me, and I worried that something was wrong and could no longer pay attention to the meeting. I knew my parents were home and I thought with all their health issues, maybe something happened to one of them. I could not wait for the meeting to be over so I could call home to find out what was going on. I could see that there were several messages on my phone, which also concerned me.

As soon as the meeting was over, I called home without even checking my messages and my mom answered. She sounded distraught and told me that they had a call from Richard's office. Something was wrong with Richard. He was at Glendale Memorial Hospital and I needed to go there right away. She also told me that because they could not get a hold of me, my sister Annie and my brother-in-law were already on their way to the hospital since their office was closer to Glendale. I panicked and I thought that I was right when I wanted Richard to go to see a doctor. He was too stressed and he probably had a heart attack. Having gone through quintuple and sextuple bypasses surgeries with my parents, I knew what was in front of us if that was the case. I was angry at him for waiting this long and I was angry at myself for not pushing him to make the change earlier but mostly I was just worried and wondered what had happened and how bad it was.

My boss was on a call, so I told his administrative assistant that my husband was in the hospital and I needed to leave right away and left. By that time, it was already rush hour and the freeway was packed and very slow moving. I was anxious to get to the hospital. Then I noticed that I was low on gas and there was no way I could make it there. I got off the freeway to get gas and as I got back in the car and back on the freeway, my sister called me. She asked me where I was, and I told her I was on the freeway but the traffic was really bad. She said they were at the hospital and I asked her what was wrong with Richard. She started crying and did not answer my question and my brother-in-law grabbed the phone from her and told me, "Arminé, everything is OK, take your time, just drive carefully, we are here, just get here as soon as you can."

I did not believe him. I knew that if my sister started to cry and could not answer me, something was terribly wrong. My heart pounded, and I trembled as I drove. I thought the worst and although my gut was telling me it was probably the worst, part of me was hoping it was just a heart attack. *Just a heart attack,* like that was nothing. Who wishes for that? I knew people survived heart attacks and could recover from them and knowing how strong Richard was, I knew he would recover if that were the case. He had been athletic and active all his life.

I started thinking about Kyle and my parents. My entire life with Richard flashed in front of me. I thought about how healthy he had been all his life, never getting sick, always exercising, taking his vitamins, eating healthy, and living a healthy lifestyle. How could something like this happen to him? I always teased him that he was in such a great shape and took care of himself so well that he was going to live much longer than me even though he was much older than me. I felt sick to my stomach, had to go to the bathroom and felt so hopeless, helpless, nervous, sad, emotional and I just wanted this to be a bump in a road, a wake-up call for him.

It took me almost two hours to get there and I found the emergency room, which was where my sister told me he was. I left my car right in the front, did not even lock it and ran inside, asked for his name and they walked me to the room where he was. The minute I saw him lying there with his eyes closed and my sister standing next to him, crying, I knew he was gone. The doctor came in and told me that he had an aortic dissection and they could not save him.

I was not even hearing anything she was telling me, I said, "That can't be, he can't just be dead, just like that. He was such a healthy person. You have made a mistake. Are you sure? Can't you do something?" I ran to the bathroom with upset stomach, throwing up and not wanting to come out to face what I had to face.

My sister Arous was there by then too. She came to the bathroom and walked me out and I wanted to hear again what the doctor had to say. I couldn't believe it. I came back to his room and I saw him lying there peacefully. I touched his face, I held his hand, I kissed him; he was still warm to the touch, but no reaction. The Richard I knew wouldn't just lie there. He would pull me down; he would kiss me, hug me, tickle me, laugh and hold me so very tight. His body was there, but his soul was no longer in that body. I was still in denial. How was I going to tell Kyle, who was only ten, that his daddy was gone? A father he so looked up to, admired and loved. He had been the fun one, when I was enforcing the rules. He had been in Trailblazers with him, coaching his soccer teams, going camping and hiking, going to the museum of science and whale watching, playing soccer and biking to the park, watching war movies and reading to him; he had been the ideal father. And now he was gone, no one could replace him or even come close, and I could never be enough for my son.

I immediately felt inadequate, guilty, and despair. My heart ached, but I was numb. I could not cry, I was still shocked and in denial. After I kissed him, hugged him and said my goodbye, I left the hospital.

By the time I got home, it was dark, late evening already. My parents were downstairs and distraught, crying. They were trying to console me, but I was frozen, I was not crying, I could not cry. I still had to face Kyle. I went upstairs and he was playing a computer game. After he hugged me, he asked me where Daddy was and why I came home so late. I could not tell him he was gone,

I just did not have the courage and maybe I was hoping that this was all a bad dream and Richard would come home from work tomorrow. I told him that he had not felt good and he had had to go to the hospital. He asked me if he was OK and I said yes, knowing that I was lying to him. I told him it was bedtime, he needed to brush his teeth, wash up, get his backpack ready and go to bed.

After he went to bed, my parents wanted to be with me, talk to me, but I just did not have any energy. I could not think, I could not hold a conversation; I just needed to be alone. I went to bed and was hoping I could sleep and wake up and everything would be different. I could not sleep, thought. I kept questioning why this happened to him, what I could have done differently, if this was a lesson for me and if so, why did Kyle and Michael have to suffer for it? I was deeply sad, sadness that I had never felt before, even when Alex and I parted. I knew I would never see Richard again. How was my life going to be now, responsible for a child and my parents? I would never feel his love again, his kisses, his hugs, his body next to mine and his abundant positive energy around us. I had lost another love and this time I was an adult, I had a child with him, and it felt so tragic, so permanent. It was the end and my life was over at the age of 38. There was emptiness and a big hole that felt like it was pulling me down.

I got up in the morning very tired, not having slept much except dozing on and off. I woke Kyle up and told him that I was going to take him to school. He asked me why because usually Richard took him to school or my parents. I told him that I was taking the day off so I can go see daddy at the hospital. I dropped him off and started thinking about how I was going to tell him when he got home. I couldn't postpone this much longer. He was sensing that something was wrong as he could tell I was sad, and I looked tired. As much as I tried to keep a normal appearance and even smile, I was not myself. And who was the right person to tell Michael? He was at Penn State at that time and it was right before Christmas break. After thinking about it, I decided it would be best if his mother called him so I decided to ask one of my family members to contact her as I was not sure I could have that conversation with her or Michael.

When Kyle got home from school, I had him sitting in my lap and told him that I had some very sad news to share with him. He asked me, "Is Daddy still sick? Is he still going to stay at the hospital?"

I said, "Honey, Daddy is gone. His heart gave up on him; he is not coming home."

He started crying, "But I am only ten years old. How can he die so early?"

It broke my heart into a million pieces. "I know honey, you only had your dad for ten years, but you had an awesome dad. Some people have dads all their lives, but they don't even spend any time with their dad or have a relationship with their dad." I don't know how much he understood that but he was crying and crying and my heart broke more for him than me. I sent him to school the following day just to keep some normalcy in his life and at the same time, not knowing really how I was going to deal with this horrible loss and how I was going to keep myself together and be strong for my ten-year-old. I was not prepared for this. Who was, at the age of 38, especially when they have a very healthy husband? How do you handle something like this? There must be some books about it.

I let the teacher know so she was aware of what Kyle was going through and left. When I went to pick him up, his teacher told me that he had been sad and teary-eyed all day and he had gotten a lot of support and love from other kids but under the circumstances, she was surprised he had been holding up and had tried to stay engaged. When we got home, Kyle showed me a note he had written which I have to this day.

God, I know you loved my dad, but I loved him more.

When I read the note, I just lost it and cried and cried and cried. I knew exactly how he felt. The following days and weeks and months were mostly a blur. I had a hard time even crying. My mom kept telling me to drink wine so I could let go and that helped, but I still had plethora of emotions. I went from denial to anger to sadness to numbness to looking for someone to blame to feeling guilty that he was gone and I was still alive. The guilt overwhelmed me. After all, Kyle was a boy and he needed his father more than me. He was the one Kyle looked up to more than me. Why was he chosen instead of me? Kyle would have been much better off with his father instead of me. I could never be like Richard, no one could; he was bigger than life.

One thing I was glad about was that Richard had lived his life to the fullest, he did not postpone truly living and being present and that was a lesson to be learned. Life was very fragile, no one knows how long he or she has and this can happen to anyone. Death does not discriminate. I told myself that I couldn't grieve forever. Life does not stop for anyone's grief and I had to pull myself together, do my best and be there for my son and my parents. I needed to be strong and set an example for my son. We talked about his father a lot, we remembered, we cried, but I always ended with the positive note that we had a guardian angel and he would want us to live our lives to the fullest and reminded myself and taught my son that life is 10% what happens to you and 90% how we react to things.

Some days I felt strong, I felt like I could do this, and I could get through this. I kept thinking about women who had lost their husbands and their sons during wars and they got through it. I thought about my grandmother who lost her husband at age 30 and lost two children later and was able to move with her other children to another country, work and take care of her children under much worse circumstances. Then there would be moments where I would completely fall apart, like when I had to take down the Christmas lights that Richard had put up. Just a few weeks ago, he had touched those same lights. Everything that reminded me of Richard brought tears to my eyes every day. The sadness and melancholy stays with you forever, when you hear a song, eat a certain food, go to a certain place, even when you find new love, even at the happiest of the moments in your life like Kyle's graduation, even today. The scar on your heart heals but the mark remains forever. As Shakieb Orgunwall wrote:

> I tried to forget you. I locked you out of my thoughts but you seem to carry a spare key. I've tried erasing your voice but every songbird sounds like it must've taken lessons from you. Every dust swirl and cloud puff paints portraits of your face. Every still stream knits quilts of your reflection on its watery skin. You were the sun and I had been staring too long. Because every time I blink, you are still all I see.

My family was at our house that Christmas and it was a very sad Christmas. Michael was almost twenty and I had hoped that a tragedy like this would strengthen the bond between him and Kyle and bring them closer but that was not in the cards. I knew he was young and it pained me that he lost his father at a very young age, but I also felt that being an older brother, he could be a male role model and support his ten-year-old brother and keep in touch when he went back to school after the holidays and during his subsequent visits. I felt that not strengthening that bond was a loss for both him and Kyle.

Unfortunately, he become even more distant and did not show much interest in strengthening that relationship. Although I did not understand him, did not really know where his mindset was, I always loved him and I always wanted him to be happy. I wanted him to know that I would always support him in any way he needed me to.

After the holidays, I went back to work and was so grateful I had a job that allowed me to at least for some moments think and focus on something other than my loss. I would come home, try to be positive and stay strong during dinner with Kyle and my parents but when I went to bed, I would break down, I had to let it out and often cried myself to sleep. Some nights, I stayed up all night, reading hundreds of cards, letters and notes he gave me over the years to feel closer to him, but instead I felt sad yet at the same time I felt so deeply loved.

At times I drank too much to numb the pain. One time I was at a friend's house and had drunk too much and the next morning I couldn't even remember how I got home. That scared me and I knew I could not continue drinking like that; I had my son to think about. He could not lose another parent. It was much easier to drink to deal with pain, lose and loneliness than to deal with my feelings, with my grief.

There were so many things I had to figure out. On the practical side, one of the most important was how I would be able to stay at the same house with one salary, to minimize disruption for Kyle and my parents. My parents depended on me, not just my son. I used my portion of the life insurance money to pay down my loan to reduce my payments and stay at the same house. I put away Kyle's portion for his future and kept it under his name and Michael got his portion and he actually also had a second life insurance which was part of his parents' divorce agreement and was to expire by age eighteen. Richard had suggested that we cancel it but I encouraged him to keep it since we could afford the premium until he at least graduated from college. When his mom found out, she was very appreciative.

Kyle took piano lessons, art lessons and played soccer and he was part of Trailblazers, which was a father son program through YMCA. I offered to be an assistant coach for soccer. I wanted him to be able to continue with the Trailblazer program at least through the end of the season since he enjoyed it so much. I asked them if they would make an exception and allow me to go with him and I was fortunate that they agreed to allow a mom to take that role under the circumstances. Here I was with a bunch of dads and boys, going rock climbing at Joshua Tree, camping at the San Diego Wild Animal Park and participating in numerous outings and activities they had. It felt a little awkward to be the only woman, but everyone was very understanding and supportive. They, too, missed Richard and it was hard at times. Although I could never take Richard's place, I think Kyle was glad that at least he got to continue with the program.

To be a mother while my heart was breaking was one of the hardest things I had to do. Life was certainly a huge adjustment and all we could do was take one day at a time and sometimes half a day at a time. I thought about summer vacation and wanted to do something special, just Kyle and me. I had always wanted to see Machu Picchu and thought that would be a very unique and spiritual experience for us, but I also wanted it to be fun, something Kyle would really enjoy. Since I knew how much he liked nature and animals, we decided on Machu Picchu and the Galapagos Islands. Our first vacation, just the two of us and it couldn't have been a better choice.

We were in Lima, in Cusco, in Machu Picchu; we hiked Huayna Picchu, visited Quito and cruised the Galapagos Island on a 90-person boat. Kyle was a trooper and although he wasn't even eleven yet, he kept up with the hiking, and thoroughly enjoyed the birds, the giant turtles and the close encounters with sea life in Galapagos. He definitely asked more questions of the guides than they were used to from an eleven-year-old. It was an amazing bonding experience for us and a deep spiritual experience for me. We very much missed Richard. Although he was not with us physically, and we missed sharing all the new experiences with him, I know he was with us in spirit, watching us all along. There was a certain lightness and ease during our trip and it seemed like all was going unexpectedly well, when it never does during trips like that. I knew Richard would have so enjoyed this vacation and I knew he was happy for us and proud of us.

Weeks and months were going by and we were adjusting the best we could, but Richard was constantly in my mind and I kept reciting a Russian poem by Lev Ozerov: "I want to think about you, I think about you. I don't want to think about you, I think about you. I want to think about others, I think about you. I don't want to think about anyone, I think about you."

Kyle did well at school, continued with his activities and I continued with my job. The following year, our big trip was to Armenia, which was something I had planned to do with Richard and Kyle after our trip to Europe. The Armenian hospitality, the beautiful sights, the warmth of the people impressed Kyle and he loved the food, especially the tomato and herb salads. I had not been back for 23 years, so it was bittersweet for me. I was excited and emotional to see my house, my school, and my city and show it to Kyle but wished Richard was there. Many places in the city reminded me of Alex and the times we had spent together. It made me wonder about how we make choices in life and why things happen the way they do. Here I was, I had lost my first love at age seventeen and my husband by the time I was thirty-eight and how was I even able to enjoy the many pleasures life offered with so much sadness deep inside me? My heart was shattered yet very much alive; I wanted to live and not just exist.

Having Kyle certainly helped me stay strong, stay positive, and have hope, faith and love in my life. I did not want to be a victim, I did not want people to feel sorry for me and I was not looking for sympathy or any special allowances from anyone. The fact was that my life was different now. My social circumstances were different. I was not part of a couple any longer and more often than not, I got excluded from couple-type activities. Married women looked at me and treated me differently now and without coming out and saying or being so obvious, there was a sense of insecurity or fear when I was around their husbands. All of a sudden, I was a threat to women and for men, an opportunity. It disappointed me to see that, especially with people who had known me for a long time. But again, I did not want to be defined or judged by my circumstances. I wanted to be treated and viewed independent of what had happened to me, but I guess that was very hard for most people.

Even at work, it almost felt that because of what had happened to me, people expected less of me or wanted to give me a break and that was the last thing I needed. If anything, work was my safe place where I knew my capabilities were not compromised. I was willing to put in more energy, more focus and more effort to subsidize for my sense of feeling less in my personal life.

We continued to travel to near and far places, which Kyle thoroughly enjoyed and embraced in addition to away summer camps he went to every year for a week or two. I loved traveling with him and watching him grow, having the opportunity to satisfy his curiosity and expand my view of the world by seeing it through his eyes. His summer camps were pure fun for him, and he often wanted to stay longer than I had signed him up for. We were fortunate to have my parents living with us, as my father was another male figure in Kyle's life. They often worked on little projects together in the garage or outside, fixed things inside the house and at times worked on bigger projects like building a professional poker table as one of Kyle's many wood working projects. Kyle loved spending time with his grandpa, going to the hardware store with him and learning how to use his tools. He also enjoyed his grandma's cooking and even got her to make the tomato herb salad he had so enjoyed when he was in Armenia. I was grateful to have my parents' support as a working single mom and I always felt that Kyle was fortunate to grow up so close to his grandparents. Not many children had that experience or the privilege.

Alex continued to keep in touch only by phone every so often. It was in the beginning of 2003 when he randomly called me just to see how I was and what was new in my life. Kyle had picked up the phone and then he handed it to me telling me it was my friend from Russia. Alex did not know that Richard had passed away and he was surprised and expressed his deepest sympathy to Kyle and me. He knew how much I loved Richard and had sensed I was very happy in my marriage. After a brief conversation, I felt he had called to tell me something but he didn't and hearing the sad news about Richard, he didn't know what else to say, which was a reaction I often got from people. We are not equipped or prepared to react to sad or bad news and don't often know what to say or how to comfort the person. I understood, I had experienced it myself.

Many years later, he told me he had called to tell me that he had moved out and was staying with his friend contemplating separation and eventually divorce from his wife. He felt it was becoming unbearable and he just could not live with her anymore. However, later he told me that his family had convinced him to stay because of his children and he had decided to try to attempt working on his relationship. He loved his children and that would have been a very hard decision for him.

Marcelo Came into My Life

As time was passing, many people encouraged me to get out, meet people, and date again. The work friend, Marcelo, who had had lunch with me the day Richard passed away, was one of them and he offered to even introduce me to some single men he knew. One day he invited me to join him and some of his friends. He said, "Come on, just go out, try it. It's a safe environment. There is a group of us going out and it's very close to where you live. I'll come pick you up if you don't want to walk in alone."

It had been about a year since Richard had passed away and I didn't think I was ready to go out or meet people. I missed him. I missed him every sing day, but he was gone and he wasn't coming back. At the same time, I wanted to move forward, go out and find some joy again. Although I had my family, my son, my friends, I still felt lonely at times and craved intimate conversations, human touch and the feelings of excitement you get when you're in a relationship.

After some hesitation and going back and forth, I said, "OK, I'll think about it and I will just drive myself, no need to pick me up." The day came and Kyle had plans for a sleepover and I missed dancing and decided I would go. I met him and his group of friends, and they were all very friendly and welcoming and tried to make me feel really comfortable. I thought he had told them ahead of time about my circumstances. I told them that this was really awkward for me as this was the first time I was going out after my husband had passed away. They were very understanding, we were all having a nice conversation, enjoying the outdoor patio and after having a drink, I started feeling more comfortable and they started to encourage me to dance and a few of us got up and started dancing. For a moment there, I surprised myself. It felt like I was betraying Richard but more than that, as much as I really wanted to dance, it did not feel right. I really didn't enjoy it, my heart was not in it. It made me feel sad, remembering how much I loved dancing with him and how much I missed dancing with him and how I would never dance with him again.

I wanted to leave but I did not want to give up so easily, be rude or make them feel sorry for me as I felt my eyes get teary. They were not too crazy about the music and decided to leave to go to another place close by where they thought there might be better dancing music. As I debated what I should do in my own head, all the discussion happened so quickly that I almost didn't even have time to think or realize what I really wanted to do and what I was feeling. I wanted to have fun, I wanted to feel good, I wanted to enjoy the evening, so without too much thought, I joined them in the second place and they did have better music and I danced again, but still, I was feeling out of place. I also felt that Marcelo looked at me differently than a friend and that made me feel uncomfortable. I was not sure I was ready for those feelings or if I was ready to be open to those feelings and I decided to leave shortly after that, and he followed me to my car.

He told me that he really liked me and wanted to get to know me better and asked me if he could see me again. I told him that I was not ready for a relationship and besides, I was too old for him, I was five years older than him and that he should find someone younger so he can have children since he didn't have any children and I had no plans to have more children at my age, as much as I loved children. I am not even sure why I brought up children; it was totally out of place. He tried to convince me not to leave yet and asked me if I wanted to go somewhere quieter but I just felt confused and was not sure what I wanted to do. I thought my safest bet was just to go home.

As I drove home, I thought it had been a mistake going out, but I also felt proud of myself for having the courage to do it. There was always a first time and regardless of when that first time was, it would always feel awkward and somewhat unnatural. Part of me felt that it was nice to be out again, dancing and realizing that others noticed me, or were attracted to me and that one day I could love again and have someone in my life who would make me feel loved and wanted and appreciated, someone who would make me laugh again and make me feel alive. I just wondered if I was dreaming or if it was really possible. After all, I had loved Richard so much. How could I ever love again like that? The hopeful romantic that I was, I felt that one should never lose hope.

In the next few weeks, Marcelo stopped by my office every so often when I worked out of the Woodland Hills office. He complimented me and told me how he really liked me. He said he'd been taking notes and had gotten to know my likes and dislikes and the kind of person I am. He was always very charming and knew exactly what to say to make me feel he really cared about me and wanted to spend more time with me. He was separated and was going through a divorce and would share stories about his relationship and make me feel empathetic toward him. He shared stories from his childhood, his brother and his sister-in-law and his parents and I was always amazed at the colorful life he had lived and yet he had not experienced much love in his family. I believed his stories and often listened to him with great interest. Over time, I started to develop an opinion about all the people in his life and I developed sympathetic feelings toward him. Later, I found out that so many of the stories he shared with me were not true at all.

We grew closer and closer as friends and he impressed me with how much he had learned about me and soon we started dating. Initially things were going well. Although our relationship progressed faster than I would have liked, I enjoyed having someone to talk to, to go out with, and to do things with. Part of me thought it was too soon, part of me really wanted to be in a relationship. We had some common interests and my friends thought he was really nice and were happy for me. He knew how to charm them; he knew exactly what he should tell each person to get them on his good side. My family, especially my parents, had their doubts though. From day one, there was something about him that they didn't quite feel comfortable with and it may have been that they saw through him better than I did. They were not emotionally involved and could see more clearly than me, and they had my best interest at heart.

I enjoyed being around him. He was fun and he was always open to doing whatever I suggested. I had so much responsibility on my own, being a single mom, working full time, dealing with my parents' health issues, feeling exhausted and drained physically and emotionally at times, that it was nice to be out with someone who was carefree, easy-going and helped me forget about the serious part of my life.

Alex called me after I had been dating Marcelo for a couple of years and I shared with him that I was dating someone. He was surprised to hear that and although he expressed that he was happy for me, he sounded tentative. In the meantime, he had moved back and was trying to work on his marriage. Again, the conversation was brief as I sensed he wasn't sure what to say or ask. The next time he called me, he asked me more questions about the person I was dating and he said, "You don't sound like you are in love with this person. I don't sense you feel the same way about him as you did about Richard. Knowing you, it surprises me that you would be in a relationship with someone you are not passionately in love with. You and I are of the same ilk. Are you sure this is the right person for you?"

I was a little perturbed at his comment. How dare he judge me from halfway around the world? He did not know me and he hadn't even seen me for more than twenty years. He proceeded to tell me that he had made the mistake of marrying his wife, because she was pregnant and he felt a sense of responsibility, even knowing she was not the right person for him. He had tried hard to make it work but did not feel that they were compatible in many ways and over time, resentment had built and whatever feelings may have been there initially, quickly dissipated.

I told him, "He is different from Richard but he is a nice guy and I enjoy his company. It's hard to be alone." It was true; I was not in love with him like I was with Richard but how could Alex tell? I had given up looking to find someone like Richard. I knew it was impossible. Alex didn't say anything else after that.

In the meantime, as my relationship with Marcelo progressed, I was cautious about introducing a new man into Kyle's life. Although outwardly he appeared interested in Kyle and expressed a desire to spend time with him, he always found an excuse as to why he couldn't show up to his games or go to the park with him or spend any one-on-one time with him. At times he seemed very selfish, finding time to play soccer every weekend and going biking but was unable to spend any time with Kyle.

There was something about him that didn't feel quite right to me, but I always thought of reasons why. I came up with excuses for him like "He has never been a parent," or "He does not know better," or "He has a different relationship with his parents than I do, he grew up with different values." I almost felt sorry for him and wanted to give him the opportunity to feel what it meant to be loved by family and to be there for each other. I often encouraged him to spend more time with his own parents and family, to be more caring and compassionate with them and I hoped that over time he would change, he would learn.

I liked entertaining and at parties, people were very attracted to him. He always offered to BBQ or prepare the drinks and made people feel good by telling them what they wanted to hear, although I didn't realize that's what he was doing initially. He would compliment women and they would flirt with him and although I felt confident enough that it did not bother me, at times it felt like he crossed the line but again I would explain it to myself: He grew up in Brazil and some of how he was acting was cultural. He was a good storyteller and always captured the attention of those around him. I became friends with some of his friends and really liked them and some of them I am friends with to this day and expect to be lifetime friends with them. I also included his family in my family's events and they were very appreciative, as they did not have any family traditions of their own. They truly liked me and often expressed how pleased they were that their son had found someone like me and enjoyed being part of my family.

He had become completely part of my life—at least the fun part of my life, not necessarily the responsibilities that came with it. I justified that in my mind by thinking that he was not my husband; these were my responsibilities, my child, my parents, and my house. I ignored it, although deep down in my heart, it did not feel right. It bothered me. I always felt that I was independent; I could take care of my responsibilities and did not need anyone and that is exactly how my parents had raised me. I did not want to acknowledge the fact that if the roles were reversed, I have done anything to help and support him without him even asking me. Being helpful, giving, generous and kind was what my parents had taught us.

I met many other men, but no one was like Richard. Just because someone was different, it did not mean I could not learn to love him and have him in my life. I felt like it was OK to settle for someone different and at least I had someone in my life when many women I knew had been struggling for many years to find someone to be in a relationship with. I didn't have a lot of time to think too much about it, or invest the time in other dates or exploring a dating site which was never something I was interested in as I believed in meeting people in more natural settings. Our relationship had sort of fallen into my lap without me making much effort and I just took it as imperfect as it was, thinking that over time, he would learn from me, from my family, and I would see some of the changes I looked for in terms of family values, responsibility and being selfless. As we all know, people don't change regardless of how much you love them, they change because they love you and want to change to be with you.

During this time, we also found out that my father had bladder cancer, which was a shock. My father had been noticing blood in his urine and he had gone to the doctor for some tests. My parents had not even shared that with us until they had the diagnosis, as they did not want to worry us. Every weekend, my parents, my sisters and I would get together in one of our homes to have coffee and talk and spend time together. We were at my sister Annie's house on a Sunday morning having coffee when they told us. All along he had cardiovascular issues and had had several surgeries, but we were not expecting cancer. We now had a new health issue to focus on. We had to meet with an oncologist to find out what his treatment options where, how much it had spread and, more importantly, what his prognosis was. After many appointments, we felt somewhat optimistic that it was contained within his bladder and there was a chance it would not spread as long as he had the appropriate treatment, which involved removal of cancer from his bladder every few months.

Loss of My Father

Marcelo and I continued dating. Life was busy with working full time and being a single parent, although my parents continued to help, even though they both continued with their health issues on and off, hospitalization, surgeries and now my father's cancer and other challenges that I had to manage as they lived with me. I was lucky to have my sisters and they were there for them too but having my parents live with me required 24/7 engagement with and attention to their everyday issues, regardless of how serious or insignificant they were.

For the initial couple of years of my father's cancer, he went to the hospital every few months for a couple of days, they would scrape off the cancer as it was contained within his bladder and had not spread, which was good news. However, at some point it spread and he had to start chemotherapy, which was brutal for him. He had a spectrum of changes after each chemotherapy, such as delusions, loss of appetite or feeling very hungry, feeling claustrophobic and at times he just wanted me to drive him around and get him out of the house. He had difficulty controlling his bathroom needs and we often had to get off the freeway quickly and look for a bathroom.

At times, he did not make it. He had accidents a few times at home when Kyle had to help him, leaving my dad feeling horrible and demoralized. His body started to ache and he didn't even want Kyle to give him a hug when he got home from school. For a man who had been our rock and always in control, he felt like he had lost control and did not want to be a burden on anyone.

From day to day, we did not know how he was going to feel, how the chemotherapy would affect him and it was very hard on my mom too who was with him all day long, while we all were at work. He did not want to go through all this, he was done living and more than once asked us if we could take him to Oregon so he could have the option of euthanasia. My mom was worried that he might do something to himself as he had a gun and she knew how determined and strong-minded my father was. At some point, we took his gun away from him without him knowing and when he found out, he was very upset and wanted to have his gun back. We tried to keep him safe but also manage his emotions, not knowing how long he had to live. After some lengthy discussions, and when he was feeling a little better, he promised that he would not do anything to harm himself and we gave him his gun back. Then he regressed again, started talking about euthanasia again and acted emotionally unstable. We wanted to take his gun away, but we could not find it anywhere. We knew he would have found some clever way to hide it but even after a thorough search, inside the house, in the garage and every place we could think of, we were not able to find it.

During the months my father had his chemotherapy treatments, Alex called me just to see how I was doing and I shared with him about my father's cancer. I thought he was probably more interested in knowing how my relationship was, but we did not even talk about that. My father's cancer was top of mind for me and I could not really focus much or concern myself with my own relationship, let alone discuss it with Alex. Even being at work, my father's illness was constantly on my mind. I would come home and the first thing I would ask my mom was about my dad. I would hear about his day, try to give her moral support, speak to my dad then attend to Kyle's needs.

Marcelo did not get much involved in dealing with my parents' health issues or Kyle's school and activities and at times, I resented that and felt that he could have supported me more. He was more interested and fully engaged when there was a party or a concert or something more fun. That should have been another sign, but then again, I had so much in my mind that I did not see many things clearly that I realized later.

My mom was very emotional during this time and often felt exhausted and helpless. For the last many months, my sisters would also stop by every day in the evenings, one then the other and they would go through the same process as I, by each asking me and my mother about my father's day, visiting with my father, debriefing about the situation or his treatment afterwards. Since I was living there, it felt like I was going through that same process three times, every day with me first and then each of my sisters. It was very draining and emotionally difficult for me. There were days when I wished I did not live there, that I could leave and go home to get a break from it. There were days when I wished my sisters did not come so I did not have to go through that process three times every day. I knew they came because they cared and loved him and they were trying to be helpful, but I was with it all the time. This was Kyle's junior year in high school and I was worried about him and how he would deal with this loss and I knew it was nearing. After all, he had already lost his father, and now another important male figure in his life was going through these health challenges and did not have much longer to live.

While we went through all this, a new job opportunity came up for me and I left my job at Health Net and started a new job at Blue Shield in April of 2007 with a higher position and even larger scope of responsibilities. It was yet another good opportunity for me to expand my skill sets and grow professionally. Of course with any new job, I had the initial learning curve and I spent longer hours to get up to speed. It was November 13, 2007, toward the end of the day and I was just about to leave the office to have dinner with our senior vice president who was visiting from San Francisco and wanted to check-in with me. It was then I got a call from my mom, crying and urging me to go home because my dad had shot himself.

I couldn't believe it. I had just taken him to City of Hope a couple of days ago for a second opinion and my father had decided to stop the chemotherapy and we were going to start hospice care at home to help him feel comfortable starting the next day. Of course, I rushed home, in shock, worried about my mom with her heart condition, worried about Kyle. *How did this happen?* When I got home, the neighbors had already called 911 and the police were there. They had taken my dad away and my mom was devastated and crying and telling me what had happened and blaming herself for leaving him to go get him Carl's Junior crosscut fries, which my dad had requested. Every so often, he craved a certain food and we always got what he wanted so he could gain some weight and feel a little stronger.

Fortunately, Kyle was not home and I did not have to deal with that at the moment. I called my friend whose son was friends with Kyle, told her what had happened and asked her if her son would invite Kyle over for dinner so I could deal with my mom and answer questions from the police. Kyle could wait until everything was cleared up in the backyard, where Dad had pulled the chair on the grass so there was no blood on the concrete and shot himself sitting on the chair. I also needed to prepare myself on how I was going to tell Kyle about this.

After the clean-up and after the police left, when Kyle came home, I told him what had happened. He was angry and sad at the same time. I felt guilty. I had brought him to this world and now not only had his father died, but six years later his grandpa committed suicide. He was the victim of my bad luck and all the challenges, pain, and suffering I was going through. I felt responsible for it. I was angry with my father at first too. *How could he do this to us? What kind of an example is this to his young grandson? Didn't he realize the impact this would have on Kyle, knowing how much he looked up to him and how close he had gotten to his grandpa?* He was the one who had given Kyle his first driving lesson. He was the one who had jumped in the Jacuzzi with Kyle for some man-to-man conversations. He was the one who had taught Kyle how to use every single tool in his garage, of which there were many. Kyle so enjoyed being with his grandpa and going to Home Depot with him. He loved his grandpa so much and looked up to him. How were we all going to move on from yet another unexpected tragedy and how was my mom going to cope after being married to him for 55 years?

Over the weeks and months, I not only forgave him, but I understood his decision and respected his courage. He had done it for us. He did not want us to take care of him; he did not want to burden us. Later, we found a string that was hanging behind a tall armoire in their bedroom where he had attached the string to the gun so no one could find it and take it away from him and his bullets were on top of the armoire, not visible unless you stood on a chair. He was very smart, and he somehow had found the physical strength to do this, even though he was so weak toward the end. Who would have thought that he would hide the gun in such an ingenious way? I always thought my father was very wise and resourceful and this was yet another example of that.

Once again, my family pulled together and gave each other strength and love as we slowly moved forward with our lives. I missed my father so much and still do. I missed our conversations and our arguments; I missed his supportive and protective nature. I missed my rock. I missed how he told me facts of life, the way they were. Even when I had hard or sensitive questions or concerns, he was always honest and authentic and explained everything with great logic. The first time I ever saw my father cry was when Richard passed away and I know he was crying for me. He tried to be strong for me every day when he saw me sad. I always felt my dad's love and support and I knew he was very proud of me and his other daughters as well. He expressed his pride in us and he was always there to help us grow, achieve, prosper and succeed in any way he could. He was compassionate when he needed to be and direct when it was appropriate. He gave us a lot of freedom to make our mistakes, but he was always there to catch us if we failed or made mistakes. He encouraged us to take chances, explore options and work hard, but have fun too. He taught us how to read manuals, how to put furniture together, how to change tires, check the oil level in the car, add water for windshield wipers and many more skills, even though we were girls. He had an unlimited capacity to make us feel confident, resourceful, capable and loved. He wanted to arm us with the truth to help us make the best possible decision. He told the truth even when I did not want to hear it, but I knew it was always from a loving and caring place. He never spoke to us in a belittling way even when we were completely wrong or had poor judgment. One time toward the end, when he was at the hospital and I was visiting him, he asked me, "Are you going to stay with Marcelo?"

I said, "Yes, we will probably get married after Kyle graduates from high school and goes to college."

He said, "You need to re-evaluate your decision. He doesn't love you. He loves what comes with you. You will not be happy with him."

I was so upset at his comment. I thought how could he hurt me like that? How could he say something like that to me when he was so ill and did not have much time left to live, instead of saying something loving to me? Why would he hurt me? Was that the last memory he wanted me to have of him? That's not how I wanted to remember my dad. I complained to my mom and she did not have much sympathy for me and sort of dismissed my concern as she probably agreed with what he had said.

A couple years later, thinking back, I knew he was right. I knew he said that to really make me think and change my mind, but I was foolish and did not want to hear what anyone had to say. I so badly missed Richard and wanted to have someone in my life. I wanted to be a part of a couple again. I did not want people to assume I was divorced when they saw me with my son and not married. I was too young for people to assume anything else and I was very sensitive to and protective of Kyle's feelings if people would say something to him based on wrong assumptions, which sometimes happened. I was tired of people asking me what had happened to my husband, how he died. I wanted people to be happy for me instead of feeling sorry for me. I wanted Kyle to feel like he was a part of a family. I did not want to be a third wheel. I did not want to be a widow anymore. There was something about that term that made me feel sad, that made me remember my loss and renewed my pain.

Challenging Years with Kyle

After my father's death, the following few years were difficult as a parent. That is when I came to realize the most rewarding experience in life was being a parent, and it is also the most challenging job in the world. Toward the end of his junior year in high school, he became more defiant, pushing his boundaries and spending time with kids who were different from his normal circle of friends. Although he was still doing well at school, he loved science and history and throughout the year he was in plays, played guitar, was on the cross country team, played soccer and played lacrosse, somehow he still found time to cross boundaries. His last year of high school and the first couple years of college were the most challenging. He experimented with drinking, smoking, marijuana and probably other drugs that I was better off not knowing about. He stayed out late, went to or hosted parties and at times I could tell he had had too much to drink, or he was high. He would be incoherent or under the influence of one vice or another—not at all what you want to see your children ever going through. I was not ready or equipped to handle this stage of parenthood. I read a lot of books, spoke with other parents and tried my best to manage these difficult times. We had not experienced any of this with Michael. Kyle was much more of a risk-taker and tested his limits, while Michael had been and still was much more risk-averse. Once again, I wished Michael was more present in Kyle's life and stayed closer to have that positive influence as an older brother.

In 2008, Marcelo and I got engaged on Valentine's Day in New York on top of Empire State Building. We were actually there for a long weekend to celebrate his 40th birthday although I had also planned a surprise birthday party for him upon our return. It should have felt romantic but it sort of felt staged. Something was missing; something did not feel authentic. Even with that gut feeling, upon our return, we started planning our wedding.

After we came back, his absences become more frequent, where he would not show up or come much later than we planned to meet or not answer my calls or text messages for a very long time. That had happened many times before, but I guess I had ignored it; I did not give it much thought, although it made me wonder. It did not feel right. I just had too much in my mind with the loss of my father, concern for my mom, working through my challenges with Kyle and adjusting to yet another new phase in our lives. He always had some explanations that felt like lies but I guess I did not want to acknowledge the truth. I ignored what my heart was telling me. We were engaged, we were planning to get married, we were looking at venues, making plans and once again my focus was on coupling, rather than seeking the truth and truly understanding myself and what I wanted or needed to be content.

One evening in July, he was supposed to come over and he did not show up. He was not answering his calls, his parents did not know where he was and the friend he was supposed to help move that evening had not seen him. He had fabricated this whole story that his friend was breaking up with his girlfriend and needed to move out right away, that his friend was emotional and he needed to help him move out and console him, and maybe take him out for drinks. I thought it was odd that the friend he supposedly was helping move had not heard from him when I contacted him. He did not mention anything about breaking up with his girlfriend or moving out. I was really upset, and I thought the worst—that all my suspicions of him cheating were true. I knew he was always very friendly with other women and often got text messages and voicemails that crossed the line. I remembered one particular woman he was talking to a lot recently and we even had been at her house for a party where she sort of ignored me and wanted to show Marcelo all the improvements she had made to her house. I could not sleep all night and decided very early the next morning to go to her house, and sure enough his car was there, parked in front of her house. I knocked and her roommate opened the door. I asked for Marcelo and she said he was not there.

I told her, "I know he is here. His car is parked right up front." She shut the door and went back inside and the next thing I saw was Marcelo coming down the street, jogging. I said, "What are you doing here?"

He said, "I am jogging."

I said, "Why would you be jogging here? This is not your neighborhood." He tried to come up with some excuse, which I did not believe. I knew he had gone out the back door, thinking he could fool me like he had many times, but it did not work this time. I was very angry but did not want to have a discussion right there. I asked him to come to my house so he could explain to me what was going on and pick up his stuff. He still tried to deny he was cheating, but I knew he had spent the night there and was trying to calm me down.

That weekend, that girl contacted me and told me that he had told her that the engagement was off, that I had returned the ring and threw him out and that he wanted to marry her and have children with her. He was lying to both of us. I told her she could have him and I suggested that the three of us get together so he can tell both of us what he wanted. I felt like she needed to know he was lying before she got into a deeper relationship with him than she already was. Later I found out that he had been running with her after work, and he had been going to a beach for picnics with her using my cooler, my chairs, my blankets. He had gone to her friend's daughter's birthday party as her boyfriend. He had been going out to dinner with her as dates. He had been living a double life.

These conversations went on for a few weeks, he was back and forth between her and me in terms of who he wanted to be with. He claimed he was confused and then decided that he really wanted to be with me and told me that he loved me, that it was a mistake and it would never happen again. I told him we should take a little time to see how things go before continuing with our wedding plans, and that we should see a therapist to understand the reason for this and also for him to understand what he truly wanted. Of course, he agreed and for a little while, he was on his best behavior. He often missed his individual therapy sessions and was not taking it very seriously. We had a couple of joint therapy sessions and he said he felt attacked by the therapist and did not want to go any more, even though he had chosen the therapist. He convinced me that he had learned from his mistake and he knew what he wanted. At that time, I should have walked away. I was hurt, I was vulnerable, we were engaged, and the wedding was being planned. I was weak, and I did not have the courage to call it off and let him go. After all he did to me and I suspected this was not the first time because it certainly was not the last time, I still went through the wedding and we got married in September of 2009.

In the meantime, Kyle had started San Francisco State in August of 2009. He came home for our wedding and was happy for me and supportive of my decision to marry Marcelo. Although Marcelo had not really made an effort to be involved in his life, Kyle had no ill feelings toward him. But then again, Kyle had no ill feelings toward anyone. He was very much like his father and accepted people as they were and now that he was going to be away at school, he was glad I had someone in my life. He just wanted me to be happy.

My challenges with him had not gone away though. When we got his grades after the first semester, I was in shock. I knew he was partying too much, but I didn't expect to see Ds, incompletes or classes he dropped. When he got home for winter break, we had a serious conversation. I was not going to pay for him to live in San Francisco and party. If he did not want to go to school, he had the right to choose that option and live with the consequences. He could move back home and work or go to trade school. It was his decision. Kyle was a late bloomer in some ways and I think part of it was that he was trying to catch up with some of the other kids and perhaps also deal with his pain over the loss of his father and grandfather. He made unhealthy choice to numb the pain. He told me he wanted to go to school and asked me to give him another chance. He said he would improve his grades in the second semester. He did improve his grades in the second semester but not by much, which resulted in probation and another contentious conversation. I made it clear that he had to improve his grades materially in the second year. He tried to explain to me that he was truly experiencing college life and asked me, "Would you rather I go through this now and get it out of my system or have a mid-life crisis when I am thirty-five?"

I did not answer but he knew what my answer would be.

Then he would follow up with another question: "Would you rather I tell you the truth or tell you what you want to hear?" He knew how important honesty was for me and knew exactly what I wanted to hear from him but somehow I had to get through to him that the decisions he made and actions he took would impact the rest of his life. Most of all, I wanted him to be safe, make good choices and be more risk-averse. Sometimes things get so difficult with your children that you really think about prioritizing what you want for them at that moment. Grades and education fall to the bottom when you are worried about their safety and, at times, whether they are alive or not. I learned that I also needed to be careful about judging his friends when he shared certain things with me. The moment you start judging them, they stop sharing and that is not what I wanted. It was a balancing act of not reacting, making suggestions but allowing them to make their choices, understanding that they are fully responsible for the consequences. I also learned that they are not always open to hearing your advice and sometimes you have to wait until they asked you.

One time I was at the airport on my way to Boston for a Strategic Negotiation program at Harvard, waiting to board my plane when I got a call from him. He sounded very emotional, probably drunk or high or perhaps both and he was telling me how it's so hard for him to have discipline, he wanted to quit school and join the Marines because he thought maybe that would help him have more self-discipline.

I did not know what to think and was very worried about him. I tried not to overreact as my heart was about to come out of my body and my blood was boiling. It was May and almost the end of the school year. I had to be very careful about what I said to him. I told him that was certainly an option, but since it was almost at the end of the school year, I suggested that he stay in school and finish the year. I told him he could always decide in the summer and not return next fall. It was not easy to convince him as he was arguing and crying. He was upset and imagine how it makes you feel as a mother. I wanted to be calm and supportive but part of me just wanted to scream at him and shake him, but I knew that would not work.

They called me for boarding and I wasn't sure if I should get on that plane or take a plane to San Francisco and be with him. As I contemplated what I should do, I could tell that he threw his phone and hit something and we were disconnected. I called back several times, but he would not answer. I got very worried. I called his friend and roommate Max and he answered. He told me Kyle broke his phone when it hit the wall, but that he was OK, he just had too much to drink and he was trying to convince Kyle to go to sleep. He assured me that he would keep an eye on him and told me he would be OK and that I could call Kyle on his phone, if I need to get in touch with him in the meantime.

I took the flight to Boston and thought that if I needed to, I could just take a flight back. As soon as we landed, I called Kyle on Max's phone. He apologized and told me that he took a nap and felt better. He assured me that he would finish the year before he made any decisions about joining the marines. I spoke with him a couple of times a day the next few days. He sounded better but it was hard to be so far away. I just had to be patient and trust that in a few weeks, he would be in a different place.

Even when he visited during the breaks or holidays, we had many trying times and I learned that ultimately, we couldn't control him. There were times when other family members judged him or reprimanded him for expressing his interest in dropping out of school to be a DJ or justifying his reasons for smoking marijuana and it made it worse when this happened during family meals and in front of non-family members by family members. That type of criticism made him defensive, and he would just leave the dinner table upset. I knew he was hurting, and I knew when people he loved did this, he felt hurt, not seen or heard. The timing of when you have those conversations and how you have those conversations is critical and it certainly should not be in front of others if you wanted him to hear you.

The public criticism by family members also made me feel awkward and defensive because it made me feel responsible as his parent when others viewed his actions to be less than acceptable. What had I done wrong in raising him? Was that a reflection on my parenting skills? You start questioning yourself and when you are a single parent, it all falls on you. Sometimes the weight of being a good parent and making the right decision was too much for me to bear. You can't always save your children and you shouldn't, but you can always be their safety net. Sometimes they just need to go through these experiences themselves, hopefully learn from them, grow from them, make better decisions, think on their own and most importantly become resourceful and self-reliant in a time of crisis. It's their life, not yours and they need to decide how they want to live and deal with the decisions they make. You can only love them unconditionally, support them, listen to them and give them advice if they want to hear it but ultimately, they need to have the privilege and the confidence to live their own life. Sometimes loving is giving them chance after chance after chance and accepting them with all their imperfections and seeing the best in them. He needed to be out there making his own mistakes but as a mother, you never stopped worrying about them and your heart still breaks when they make mistakes and you so badly want to protect them. I really wished Kyle and Michael were closer and he could have had his brother's support during these challenging times but not much had changed in their relationship.

Over the years, Kyle slowly matured and in some ways I saw great changes in him and continued to see him grow and I knew that he was doing it on his own because he wanted to and that alone was the beauty. He was walking his path, not mine or anyone else's.

After Marcelo and I married, the times we were out together or we traveled or attended any type of function were good. We had fun; he was easy to be with and always open for new experiences. But that's not the most important part of life. Most of life is routine and he was not reliable or responsible. He was lazy and selfish, and he often lied to me about unimportant things. Since we were married now, I expected a different level of commitment, partnership and sharing responsibilities, both financial and non-financial. But that was not what happened. In fact, maybe because we were married now, he made even less effort and still behaved like a guest, as a date, as someone who came and went as he pleased and focused on his needs and interests. There were times when we would host a party and his friends and parents were invited and he would go on a long bike ride, leaving me to prepare for everything. He would have the audacity to call me when he had a flat tire to go pick him up right in the middle of my preparation. Sometimes, he would show up right when the guests were arriving, take a quick shower and pretend that he had been there all along, preparing with me. He regressed back to his old ways and even worse, once we were married. I became more and more resentful and could not rely on him or trust him, and our relationship slowly deteriorated. He had conned me and he would never change.

Alex in Moscow

I t was January 1, 2010 when Alex called me to wish me a Happy New Year. He also shared with me that he had gotten divorced in 2008 and now he was living and working in Moscow although during that call he was in Tambov visiting his children. He and his wife had a friendly relationship and in fact, she was next to him and she also wanted to wish me a Happy New Year. She was very nice on the phone and told me, "Alex has always talked about you and I have heard great things about you. I felt like all my life I had to measure up to you and I know you have been good friends for a long time. We still have the painting you had gifted Alex when you were sixteen hanging from our living room. I hope I get to meet you one day."

I was surprised at her comments and told her that I had heard wonderful things about her from Alex and wished her a Happy New Year. When Alex got back on the phone, he asked me how my relationship was going and he was speechless when I told him I had gotten married. He congratulated me which did not feel sincere and then he was quiet for a while and then told me he was surprised. He repeated once again that when I talk about Marcelo, he did not get the sense that I am in love or that he was the right person for me. He was disappointed and surprised I had made that choice. Then he said, "My kids are waiting for me, I have to go. I'll call you another time; we need to talk." He hung up. It felt like some things were left unsaid once again.

A few months prior to this conversation, one of my classmates from Armenia who lived in Washington, DC had told me about this Russian website where you could find your classmates based on the school you went to. She said many of our classmates from Yerevan, Moscow and the US were on that website and were planning a 30-year reunion in Moscow in May of 2010 and I should join the group chat. I hadn't had a chance to check out the website but sometime early in 2010, I wanted to see which one of our friends I could find and the idea of a 30-year reunion sounded intriguing. Once I signed on, it was nice to connect with many that I had not kept in touch with for 30 years. Through the group chat, many were really supportive of the reunion and the excitement was building up over the next few weeks. Given where I was in my personal life, I thought it might be good for me to get away, catch up with my friends and reminisce about our childhood. I decided to go to Moscow for the reunion for a week. Once I told them I was going to be there, many were very excited and Alex messaged me through the website indicating that he couldn't believe I was going and saying how anxious he was to see me after 30 years when he thought he would never ever see me again, especially since I had gotten remarried.

We kept in touch through this website over the next few months and he updated me about some of our friends who were going to be at the reunion as he had kept in touch with some of them through the years. As it got closer to my departure date, I asked him what the best options would be for transportation from the airport to the hotel. He told me that although he did not drive because there was no need for it in Moscow with very efficient metro system, he would like to pick me up from the airport with his nephew who had a car and they would take me to my hotel. I was going to arrive the day before the festivities were going to start. Marcelo was supportive of me going and thought it would be fun for me to reconnect with my friends after 30 years. Surprisingly, he did not express interest in going and I had told him that he could go if he wanted to with the understanding that my friends and I would be mostly speaking Russian and Armenian and at times, he may have to find things to entertain himself since I would be spending a lot of time with my friends. He said he did not feel comfortable venturing on his own in Russia and he did not want me to feel pressure to translate or entertain him, which I thought was very understanding of him but at the same time, it almost felt like he was looking forward to me being away. Truthfully, as it turned out, no one's partner participated in the festivities even though some of them lived in Moscow.

I was nervous and excited at the same time to see my friends, including Alex. Once I arrived, I went through customs, feeling butterflies in my stomach, feeling tired and anxious at the same time. I had not seen any of my friends for 30 years. I had not been back in Moscow for over 30 years. So many emotions and thoughts went through my mind. I was not sure what to expect. I started looking for Alex. I almost did not recognize him. I may not have found him if he hadn't called out my name. He looked changed, he looked terrible, and he looked much older than his age. He looked thin and unhealthy, ashy skin, some of his teeth were missing and soon I learned that he smoked and drank excessively. I was in shock to see how much the good-looking guy I had left behind 30 years ago had changed.

He had a big bouquet of field daisies for me, which he remembered were one of my favorite flowers after tulips. He had remembered that and said by May, they didn't have tulips anymore so he had to settle for daisies. It was so sad for me to see him so changed that it almost brought tears to my eyes. He used to be very handsome and athletic. He took good care of himself, was full of energy and always had nice color on his face. We both sat in the back of the car as his nephew drove us to the hotel and we talked about our children and our friends we were going to see the next day. We talked about Los Angeles, Moscow and Yerevan. He still had the same eyes, deep, dark and penetrating and the same warm smile and loud laugh so contagious and from his heart.

As I checked in at the hotel, he suggested that we go get some dinner and said it would be "safer" if I went with him rather than on my own, although I was staying in the center of the city in a safe area and a very nice hotel. He jokingly said during the duration of my stay, he was planning to be my bodyguard, just like in the movie *Bodyguard*, although looking at him physically I looked stronger than he did. I asked him to give me some time to freshen up and we could go, as I was hungry and needed to eat something.

We walked over to a nearby restaurant, had a nice meal and it was enjoyable to remember our school years and talk about our past and present. As we sat outside, Alex drank vodka and smoked cigarettes throughout our dinner and when I commented about his smoking, he became very defensive and said that that's one thing he cannot change nor does he want to. I asked him, "Why didn't you and your wife ever move to the US to give your children better opportunities and for a better life for you two? Your father-in-law lives there and could sponsor you."

He said, "I was never interested in moving to the US. My children are into classical music and art and they would probably end up driving taxis in America. That country does not appreciate or support people in the arts. They care more about athletes, actors, businessmen, money and materialism and as you know, that's far from my values."

I was not surprised at his response and I couldn't say I disagreed with his observation. I knew many friends of my parents who were musicians, artists and historians and many of them did not have jobs in their fields. We discussed a little more about the positive and negative aspects of the US and Russia and after a while, he said, "You have not changed Arminé. You have the same soul. I thought that country would have changed you. It changes many people. I am pleasantly surprised and so happy for that." I was a little offended that he expected the core of who I am would change.

I said, "You have changed. Look at you. You look terrible. What are you doing with your life? Are you in self-destruction mode?"

He said, "When you have no love in your life, life is not worth living."

I said, "How about your children? You need to be there for them; they are your life. You also have your brother and sisters and their families."

He said, "No one needs me, no one understands me, it's a lonely life. Even in this country, people have different values and priorities now. Look at Moscow; it's like any western city. Everyone just cares about material things; humanity is lost. It has changed a lot since you left."

I felt deep sorrow for him and encouraged him to reevaluate his views. I told him that his children needed him, they needed his values, his influence, and they needed his love and support. After dinner he walked me back to the hotel and he took the metro home. We agreed that he would come pick me up the next morning. We would do some site-seeing before we met up with our friends in the evening.

He came by in the morning with more flowers. I told him I didn't have another vase in the room for the flowers and he asked the hotel to give me another vase. Every day I was there, he brought me different flowers and asked for another vase. We had some coffee and light breakfast at the hotel and then I wanted to walk in the city, take the metro, go to Gorky Park, go to Red Square, visit the churches, monuments and museums, go down the Moscow river on the boat, see a performance at the Bolshoi theatre, and eat authentic Russian food. Although we couldn't do all that while I was there, we were able to see quite a bit.

The next few days I had an amazing time with my friends. It was like the old times, we walked around the city every day, we spent time in cafes and restaurants. We ate, we drank, most of them smoked, we reminisced, we laughed, we cried, we danced and most of all, we felt immense nostalgia. It felt really good to reconnect after thirty years. Alex was really having a great time and if I could just ignore how he looked, he was the same person I knew thirty years ago. He was still full of fire, full of passion, full of idealism. He still had a gentle soul and kind heart, and I told him so. He said it was only because I was there and he wouldn't even go to the reunion if I wasn't going to be there.

Unlike typical reunions, this reunion was not just one big party. It was just different activities throughout the week. After a couple of days, I lost my voice completely. There are many poplar trees in Moscow that bloom in May/June and all the bloom from the trees was giving me an allergic reaction, which I had never had before. Not only had I lost my voice, but my eyes were also red and watery. I was not sure if it was from the trees, all the late nights, all the drinking, all the smoking around me or just talking and laughing too much. It was getting worse and by mid-week, I decided I needed to get back. Alex begrudgingly helped me find a ticketing office in the city where I could change my flights back. He was upset that I wanted to leave early. He had even gotten tickets for the Bolshoi to see a ballet but it was Friday and I was returning on Thursday. He said, "I have so much more to tell you. I wanted all this reunion excitement to die down so you could focus on what I have to say."

I said, "You can tell me now, or you can tell me over the phone."

He said, "Once again I am losing you."

I said, "What do you mean once again? I am married, you did not have me again."

He had tears in his eyes as he gently hugged me and said, "You'll see, you have made a mistake. He is not the right person for you. I can see it in your eyes, I can sense it when you talk about him. I don't feel joy in your heart. He will not make you happy."

I left the next day. His nephew drove us to the airport and as we were parting, I leaned to give Alex a hug and he said, "Just go. I don't like long goodbyes." I gave him a quick hug and walked away. Then he called after me, "Why are you leaving so fast?"

I said, "You said go."

He said, "Yes, but I didn't mean it, come back, I need another hug before you go as I may never see you again or at least not for another thirty years."

I said, "Don't be so pessimistic, you need to come visit me the next time. You even have a nephew who lives in Los Angeles. You can stay with him." We said our goodbyes and I walked away to catch my flight. Part of me did not want to leave but I knew I needed to leave; I had a hard time breathing, my eyes were getting worse and I did not want to hear one more time that I had made a mistake—although deep down in my heart, I knew he was right.

At the end of summer that year, Alex went to Armenia to visit his sister and to attend a cousin's wedding. Whenever he, his brother or his sister from Ukraine visited Yerevan, they stayed at his parents' house, which still looked the same way it had many years ago when he had moved to Russia. No one lived there, as his other sister had her own apartment in Yerevan. He had called me from Armenia to tell me how annoyed he was with his sisters, because they were trying to set him up with a girl who was also attending the wedding and I told him he should be open to it. He also told me that he had found my diary at his parents' house in the bookcase in his room, where he left it thirty years ago. He had left it behind thinking it would be safer as he did not want his wife to find it back then and ask him to destroy it. I cannot even describe the overwhelming emotions I felt when he told me that he still had my diary and he would give it to me when we saw each other again. I was in disbelief and speechless. I so badly wanted to see it, read it. I was not sure if I would ever see him again and I was too impatient so I asked him to write me an email with the content of my diary, every day for a few days, and he did until I got it back. I so enjoyed reading my diary and it brought back so many memories. I did not want it to end and wished that I had written more.

Life Lesson

I got home and my mood instantly changed. Marcelo didn't even look excited that I was back or show any true signs of missing me. He said the right things, but it sounded so insincere. I could see right through him. The exhilaration I had felt in Moscow was gone. I felt despair and now I had to figure out what I was going to do with my life. The next few months were very trying and progressively got worse. He would say what he thought I wanted to hear but his actions did not support them. This relationship was not working for me. Marcelo was never going to change and one time he even asked me, "Why do you have such a big problem just because I had an affair? When my father was working in Venezuela, he had a girlfriend and my mom knew about it and she never cared."

I said, "I am not your mother. That does not work for me." Even after we were married, his disappearing acts continued. He acted like he was not doing anything wrong. He continued to lie and his callousness about how I felt about his actions became intolerable.

As time went by, I became more and more resentful of him and even when we were on vacations together or at fun events, the way

I interacted with him or reacted to him was not kind and loving and reflected my unhappiness with him. The worst part was not even the constant trust issues I had with him, his selfishness or my growing resentment. The worst part was I did not like who I had become and it had spread to other parts of my life. I did not like that I had lowered my standards, I had compromised my values, I was not honest to myself or to others, just to preserve this relationship. From the outside, maybe most people could not see the continuous deterioration of the relationship, or maybe they could but did not want to say anything, but preserving the relationship was not making me happy. In fact, over time, it was getting worse. I was not living an authentic life true to my values and beliefs and I learned that when you make decisions out of fear, it never works, you are never content and the situation either needs to end or you live with misery the rest of your life.

Marcelo came home after work one evening and I was sitting outside in the backyard, it was a warm day and I had started eating dinner since he was late once again with no explanation. I was upset and all kinds of thoughts went through my mind, wondering where he was and why wasn't he answering his phone once again or responding to my test messages. He noticed that I was upset and had tears in my eyes and asked me why. I snapped, asking him, "Do you even have to ask that?" I proceeded to tell him that he was late again with no explanation other than he was working late, but he did not answer his phone nor did he respond to my text messages.

He said, "What does it matter? I am home now, aren't I? Why are you upset about that?" He just did not get it. I had trust issues with him already and felt that he was not doing anything to improve that nor did he care. On the contrary, his actions were making it worse and I knew things would not improve, they would just get worse over time. I chose to end the misery and filed for a divorce in June of 2011. I realized that I needed to live my life for myself and not worry about what other people would think. Marrying him even after dating for several years, especially knowing but not acknowledging who he truly was, was a mistake. Filing for a divorce less than two years later was the right decision to end my misery and it felt right. He was surprised by my action since I had forgiven him before and had put up with things that, when I look back, still made me angry. He told me he would try harder to change and I told him divorce takes six months and I can always pull the papers if I truly believed he had changed. I can't believe I even said that because people fundamentally don't change but I still felt that maybe there was a small chance. Even when we know we need to let go of things, sometimes it's very hard to actually do it. I knew I would just be prolonging my misery if he did change temporarily and convinced me to change my mind. I am so glad he did not continue making promises because I felt like I was in such vulnerable position and wanted this to work so badly, that I may have agreed, even though cognitively I knew I should not. He never even truly tried, and he certainly never changed. I asked him to move out, but he was not taking any action and he was telling me he had no place to move. Even his parents called me and told me, "He is stupid for losing someone like you. We don't want him to move back home with us again."

I told them, "Then you need to tell him that. He cannot stay here. He needs to rent an apartment." I went to New York for few days in August, just to be alone and clear my head because at times, I still doubted myself, I was not sure what I really wanted, I was not sure if I was doing the right thing and the few days I was gone, he never called me or texted me to see how I was. I realized that he didn't really care about me, as my father said, he just did not want to give up what came with me.

He did not move out all summer, telling me he was looking for a place. Some days he would not come home and I know now that he was probably with one girl or another. In fact, he ended up having a baby with one of them, but never married her as she too kicked him out of the apartment because he was cheating on her as well. He continued to cheat on many more after that. To this day, that pattern continues, and he is still selfish, irresponsible, cowardly, and inauthentic. I actually felt sorry for him, for being such a lost soul and not having the ability to love, to give, to care, to be kind, to be content. He had no one to go to when he was having difficult times even for years after we separated. He called me when his grandmother died, when his girlfriend cheated on him with his brother, and every other time there was drama in his life. I would hear him out, I would let him cry on my shoulder, and I would try to help him by being empathetic and giving him advice. I felt sorry for him. Many of my friends thought I was a fool for being there for him and that I was too kind to someone who had hurt me so many times.

In September of 2011, I told him that I was going away for a girls' weekend with my friends and I needed him to move out by the time I came home. He had mostly moved out when I got back except a few things and he used that as an excuse to come back and see me, but I told him I did not want him back in my house. I had helped Marcelo get a job at Blue Shield a few months after I had started there and we worked in the same building but different floors, different departments. It felt uncomfortable and awkward for me to drop off his things by his desk, so I told him that he could meet me in the parking lot and I gave him the remaining items he had left at my house a few weeks later.

I could not even stand seeing him or being in the same room with him and often I declined invitations by our common friends for that reason. At times I ran into him at work and I felt angry and resentful that I had married him. At times he would stop by my office to speak to me like nothing had happened, he would be back to his conniving ways, trying to impress me or get me to soften toward him. I had so much anger in me toward him that it was not possible. I finally saw right through him.

In October of 2011, I went to Armenia with Habitat for Humanity to build homes. I needed to be away, and I wanted to focus on doing something for others to help deal with my failure and think through my decision. When Alex found out I was going to Armenia for Habitat for Humanity, he joined the group too. When I told him that I had filed for a divorce, he felt bad for me but told me I was going to be OK and I had made a good decision and not to feel bad. He was empathetic and I could tell part of him was happy. I appreciated his support but I was not ready to feel good or right about it and I certainly resented that he expected this would happen and he told me so and I just chose to resist the truth. I told him things might still change and I had just filed and not divorced Marcelo yet and as much as I could tell he wanted to tell me I was crazy, he acknowledged my feelings and said he supported me and just wanted me to be happy, regardless of what I decided.

Building homes for over a week in Armenia and facing the challenges others have in their lives was really good for my soul. I got such great satisfaction to be able to give back to my motherland and see the smiles. The gratitude of the family we were building for really lifted my spirit. I had time to really think through things while I was far away and doing physical work in a new and different environment. I acknowledged that divorce is a loss, a loss of a relationship, loss of belonging and feeling of failure, even when it's the right thing to do and I initiated the divorce. I blamed myself for making such a mistake and I felt guilty that once again, I had put my son and my family through my drama, through my trauma and it was not fair to them. As much as I believed that I had done the right thing, part of me wished that it had worked out. Part of me wished that I would come back, and Marcelo would miraculously be a new and different person.

When I got back, Marcelo called me and wanted to meet me for coffee. As much as I didn't think it was a good idea, part of me could not resist so I agreed to meet with him. I thought he was going to be remorseful, apologize, ask me to take him back, promise me he would change once again and was I ever wrong. He started off by saying, "It's been really hard you know." When he said that, I thought he was missing me and wanted us to get back together. Then he said, "You know, I am in this empty apartment, with just a mattress on the floor, no furniture, no TV, I have to buy everything, start over."

That's when I lost it. I said, "That's what is hard for you? Really? When you got married the first time, your father-in-law bought you a house and everything that came with it. Before that, you lived with your parents; after you got divorced from your first wife, you lived with your parents for free and did not contribute anything. Then you moved in with me and barely contributed anything. You never had to buy anything yourself, and now for the first time in your forties you are going to live on your own and actually have to furnish your apartment and you think that's hard?"

I just got up and walked away, and for the first time, I accepted that he did not know how to love, he was just not capable of loving. He never loved his parents or brother, he never loved any woman or me in his life and he never would. He was a selfish, pathological liar and a narcissist. For the first time, I was sure that this was the right decision and living an authentic life gave you power and although I may have thought this was a mistake, it was also a good lesson. I now knew that I could not settle for anyone just to be in a relationship and I had to live a life true to myself. I would never compromise my values and if I wanted to be content and happy. I had learned that there was nothing lonelier than feeling alone inside a marriage. Sometimes you grow the most at your lowest point in life.

Although I had shared with my family and Kyle that Marcelo and I had some challenges and I did not think we were going to be able to work things out, I was not sure I had come across confident or made it clear that my decision was final. At this point, I felt like I needed to share with them that my decision was final and that the divorce was immanent, which I did. Although they were sad and disappointed for me, they were supportive and I sensed they were OK with it, as they never really completely liked him. With Kyle, I had to have a little more in-depth conversation so he understood why adults sometimes made wrong decisions and had to correct them even though it was painful and not an ideal outcome when it came to marriage. As I expected, he understood and he too was supportive and once again, just wanted me to be happy.

Our divorce was final in December of 2011. Many people were surprised when they heard about our divorce. What the outside world sees often can be very different from the reality and it's very easy for people to be deceived, whether it's intentional or not. Of course, my side of the story afterwards was very different than his side of the story and his side of the story changed depending on whom he was telling the story to. Over a year after we were divorced, he wanted to meet with me again, as he often did to share yet another drama he was having. At that point, he had broken up with his baby's mom. As angry as I was toward him, I decided that when I met with him, I needed to let him know that I forgave him, not because what he did to me was OK, but because I wanted to move forward and let go of that anger. When you forgive, you don't change the past, but you change the future.

When he heard I forgave him, he thought he had a chance to rekindle things with me, but I quickly explained that was no longer possible. I forgave him for myself, not him, but I still felt the pain, the disappointment, the failure, and the loss. I had been single, married, widowed and now divorced. Every time I had to complete a doctor's form, I was not sure which box I should check. I don't know why all that mattered to me but at the time, it did and maybe it was the fear of who I was without anyone in my life. Only later in life did I learn that the power came from being by yourself, independent, not needing anyone, feeling confident and knowing that I could do anything I wanted, all was good and life was beautiful. My life experiences and traveling alone taught me that it was only when I was alone that I truly felt the power. I learned that I needed to figure out who I was and who I wanted to be, not who my parents wanted me to be, or who others expected me to be. I learned that I needed to walk my path, not someone else's path.

Alex Again

---

lex had called me few days after my divorce was final and
I shared with him the deep sadness I felt for my failure,
even though I knew the divorce was the right thing. He
suggested that I go to Moscow for New Years, enjoy a Russian New
Year's Celebration with the snow, music, parties, fireworks and
which in some ways was more festive than Christmas in the US.
I didn't really want to stay home and think about Marcelo or my
divorce and thought getting away might be a good idea, so I took
a flight on December 30th and was in Moscow for New Year's Eve.

It had been a while since I had last seen Alex. He looked
different. He had grown a beard, which was mostly gray and
made him look a bit older, but he somehow looked more refreshed
and he seemed to have a different energy around him—more
positive, more hopeful. He was very happy to see me and to
have the opportunity to spend New Year's Eve with me. There
was an old belief in our culture that says: *The way you spend
your New Year's Eve is how you will spend the rest of the year.*
Of course Alex reminded me of that and wanted to make sure
we had a fun time. We went out to dinner, where they also had
dancing and shortly before midnight, we went to the Red Square

to see the fireworks. It snowed lightly and with all the lights and decorations, the Red Square looked spectacular despite it being very crowded with people and performers. We spent some time there, walking around, enjoying the celebrations and then returned to my hotel for a late-night drink. He reminded my how much we both liked Pablo Neruda's poem *If You Forget Me* and we still remembered some of the lines. We talked about Paulo Coelho's *The Alchemist* and about *Love in the Time of Cholera* (which I loved) and *One Hundred Years of Solitude* (which he had read twice and I never could finish it) by Gabriel Garcia Marquez. Neither one of us enjoyed small talk but could stay up all night for a deep philosophical conversation—the kind we both craved, filled with raw passion and intimacy, the kind that was honest and vulnerable, the kind that touches every piece of your soul and shakes you from your core—and that's exactly what we did that night.

The next day, Alex wanted to have a serious and more practical conversation. He said, "I have dreamed about this day for over thirty years now. I really want to spend whatever remaining life I have with you. I don't have to date you, or get to know you. I just want to marry you because I have loved you all my life and I can't lose you again or give you another opportunity to marry someone else again." Alex always knew what he wanted and he had the courage to express his feelings without playing any games or playing it safe. He was not afraid to be vulnerable and for the people he loved, he would go to the end of the world. He didn't have to say anything to me. I felt his love every time I spoke with him, but I was not ready for this commitment yet, as much as my heart found comfort whenever I spoke with him on the phone, or Skyped or emailed or when I was with him. I also knew that we lived in very different worlds. He never wanted to go to the US and I could never live in Russian any more.

I told him, "I cherish our friendship very much and would not ever want to lose it, but it's too soon for me to make this kind of decision. I don't know if it's possible for us to be together. I live in the US and you live in Russia. We have our lives, our jobs, our children, our families."

He said, "I have thought about it. I knew you would not move to Russia. I'll move to the US, then petition for my children."

I had not even met his children yet at this time and was not sure how it all was going to work out or if they would even want to move to the US or how their mother would feel about it.

I said, "But you don't even like the US."

He responded, "You are right, I don't, but I am not moving to the US because I like the US. I want to be with you. I don't care where you live. Even if you lived in Kathmandu, I would move there." He gave me a ring with a panther design and an emerald stone, which is my birthstone, and said, "This is not really an engagement ring, this is yet another promise ring. I want you to really think about it. Don't break my heart again."

I asked him about the panther design and he said: "Remember the panther in the zoo in Yerevan, when we were sixteen? I still think you are like a panther with a very calm disposition, purposeful walk, flowing moves like you are contemplating your next move and your gaze allows me to see the depth of you."

The next few days, he was off from work, so we spent a lot of time together walking around the city, eating our favorite foods and reminiscing. It was like being back home with my favorite friend who could finish my sentences, could sense my moods, and guess my thoughts. Without even me realizing, I was sharing my deepest feelings. It was almost like he knew me better than I knew myself.

After my beautiful week there, I returned with thoughts of what I should do. I did not want to make another mistake by jumping into another relationship, yet his energy really pulled me toward him. There was something very comforting, familiar and alive being with him. His warmth, his gentleness and his passion were hard to ignore. When I returned, he contacted me right away and wanted to know what I thought, and I told him that I needed some time to think about it and I needed not to have any contact with him for a few weeks so I could think things through clearly. He was not happy to hear that, but he understood and told me to take whatever time I needed, if that was going to help me decide.

It was very hard not to keep in touch with him. He had become a good friend and a necessary presence in my life, and I felt a strong need to interact with him every day. I would go on the Classmates website and see that he was on, but I didn't chat or write to him. I think he could see I was on and he would post songs that we both knew and with words that expressed his feelings. He knew I did not want him to write to me, call me or chat with me, yet he was communicating in a way through the songs he was posting. That was so Alex, so him, and he knew he could get through to me and he knew I was the forever hopeful romantic and these songs meant something to me, exactly what he wanted them to mean to me.

It was a difficult two to three weeks not communicating with him, especially hearing the songs and knowing he was just on the other end of the Internet. I didn't need to see him or talk to him. Knowing that he existed in the world, even half way around the world, breathing with me and feeling and thinking what I was feeling and thinking was enough. I did not need anything more. My heart told me not to deny my desire and to take another chance at love, however unrealistic it appeared; yet my head told me it was not a good idea, especially since my last experience. I was much more hesitant to jump into another relationship so quickly. But this was not just another relationship. This was the love I had given up as a teenager being logical and listening to my head. Did I really want to do that again and not follow my heart? I was nearing 50 and I was not sure if I was going to have many more chances at love. At the same time, I knew this was a big risk. Taking the responsibility where someone was going to move half way around the world to be with me, leaving his job, his children, his family behind was not something people did easily, but most people didn't get a chance at this type of love. What if he didn't like it here, what if things did not work out, what if this was just an illusion for both of us, trying to fulfill a childhood dream?

I also was aware that Alex had some health challenges. But when does love ever have any guarantees even with normal circumstances? I knew that better than anyone. I had learned that it was better to love and lose than not love at all. I believed that anything truly worthwhile in life did not come easy. I also knew, it was much harder for me to truly connect with people at a deeper level unless there was true love and I was not interested in just finding someone who could check all the normal boxes people looked for these days for a relationship. Alex gave me that opportunity, another chance at a great love, after more than 30 years of being apart. This must have been meant to be. I decided I was going to take the chance.

Soon after I found an immigration lawyer and started the paperwork to legally sponsor him with a fiancé visa for him to move to the US. Many questioned my judgment and my decision, including some members of my family, which made the process uncomfortable and difficult at times. My brother-in-law asked me, "You can't find anyone in the Los Angeles area with population of thirteen million so you are going to bring someone from Moscow that you hardly know?"

I asked him, "Do you know anyone you think would be a good match for me?" There was no response.

My mom, in general, often questioned my judgment and decisions in life. She always thought I thought too much with my heart instead of my head, I trusted too much, I just wanted to have fun; people wanted to take advantage of me and questioned why a smart woman like me would not use her head to make life's most important decisions. For her, it was important to check the boxes and if someone looked good on paper, then that was a better match than falling in love with someone without checking the boxes. She never accepted the fact that I was never the "checking off the boxes" type of person regardless of what the circumstances were, in love or in other matters. If I'm going to get hurt because I thought with my heart, then so be it. I believed in being all in, giving my all and I had come to a point where I was OK if things don't always work out perfectly. I had learned that true love was loving people with all their imperfections. It's easy to think you love someone when everything is perfect. To me, it came down to values and deep connection. I believed it was more important to want to be with someone because you loved them deeply rather than needing someone. Many times when it was just my mom and I and we talked about love, I shared stories or my feelings or I would have her listen to certain songs and expressed my astonishment at having such profound feelings. She often did not seem to even comprehend what I was talking about. She even told me one time that she had never felt about anyone the way I feel or express myself when it came to love. It was sad for me to hear that, but I did not stop sharing my thoughts or feelings with her. I always hoped that one day she would understand me; she would appreciate me for who I was and how I felt, even if it meant I kept making mistakes in life.

Even when I was very young, I always felt that unless I achieved perfection, I was not good enough. If I had all A's and one B, she would focus on the B and tell me I did not work hard enough. If I cleaned the windows and 98% of the window was clean but the corner may have not been perfectly clean, she would focus on that. She did not believe in praising her daughters because she thought they would get spoiled. It was important for her that we had strong work ethics and we were disciplined. Our housed was always clean and everything was organized and in its place. Regardless of what I had achieved in other aspects of my life, I always felt I was not good enough for her because I made mistakes, I had friends who in some ways were not up to her standards, and I made my decision with my heart and not my head which sometimes resulted in me getting hurt. It bothered her more than it bothered me and all I wanted was to feel her unconditional love and know that she was proud of me. She saw me as her extension. She was so good at so many things and she wanted me to be good at the same things she was but I was my own person, different from her and how I viewed the world. I was like her in some ways, but I was much more like my father in many other ways. She even once asked, "How can one be so much like her father?" as it manifested into same disagreements that she had with my father. I believe she loved me in her own way and I had to come to a realization that how she viewed me or what she wanted for me was not about me or who I was, it was more about her and what she wanted for me. I knew she came from a place of love, the way she defined it. I knew I would not be the person I am today if I didn't have the life experiences I had based on the choices I made in life.

The Long Waiting Process

When I told Alex about my decision, he was ecstatic, and he could not express himself enough with words how happy he was that we were finally going to be together. Soon after we started with the paperwork, Alex was hospitalized with heart issues. After some tests, it was determined that he had had a heart attack. He needed to change his lifestyle, he needed to take medication and he kept reassuring me that he was feeling fine and he was drinking less, eating healthier and he was reducing his smoking. It was so hard being so far away from him to truly know how he was, how serious his condition was. Was he telling me the truth and was he really looking after himself? After a few days he got out of the hospital and we wrote each other every day and Skyped almost every day and at times, it was difficult with the time difference and our work schedules, but we tried our best. Sometimes it was amazing how much more you can express about your feelings when you are writing to someone rather than speaking to them. Within a couple of years, we had around 1,000 pages of written communication to each other back and forth.

Even with all that written and Skype communication, we were feeling that it was not enough. We had a great need to be with each other physically. There was no knowing how long the process would take, until he had an approval to move to the US. Every so often, either he or I needed to send updated paperwork or new forms to the lawyers and just wait in between. His health seemed to be OK as he took medication for it and he felt comfortable and strong enough to travel. We decided that maybe while we were going through the process and waiting, we could meet in countries where there were no visa requirements for him to make it easier to travel.

We visited countries such as Croatia, Ukraine and Israel and I also visited him in Moscow. All our trips were amazingly romantic, felt very short, full of excitement and passion and some with adventure. It felt like I was with someone I had known all my life. Theoretically I had, but there was a gap of 30 years where we didn't see each other.

On one of our trips, I met him in Moscow and I there less than 24 hours before we flew to Israel for a week. After Israel, we returned to Moscow for a few days to visit with his children, and then flew to Dnepropetrovsk, Ukraine to visit his sister. On the way back from Ukraine, my flight had a stop-over in Moscow before returning to LA. I arrived in Moscow at night and we left for Israel the next morning. As we went through customs in Moscow, the Israeli customs officer asked us many questions around the purpose of our travel, how we knew each other, why was I traveling through Moscow, questioning why we were traveling together but were residents of different countries. We briefly told him our story and hoped that it would explain our unusual circumstances and we were happy we were able to get through customs and travel on to Israel. The questioning felt much more extensive than I had ever experienced before.

We very much enjoyed our trip. We stayed in Tel-Aviv, but visited a few sites such as the Masada, the Wailing Wall, and the Dead Sea and even visited the Armenian Quarter in Jerusalem. When we returned from Israel to Moscow, customs did not allow me to stay in Moscow. They told me that I needed a multi-visit visa and I only had a single visit visa. I didn't realize that I needed a multi-visit visa since the first time I was there for less than 24 hours before we flew out to Israel and returning from Ukraine was only going to be a transfer. I asked them if I could pay to get an expedited multi-visit visa, but they refused. They pulled me into the immigration office, questioned me extensively and told me that Israel should have never let me get on the plane to return to Russia and that I could not stay in Moscow. They said I could either go back to Israel or since I had plans to go to Ukraine in a few days, they could send me directly to Ukraine that day and Alex and I would have to purchase new tickets since the ones we had were for a different day. It was disappointing to miss my opportunity to stay in Moscow for few days and the chance to spend time with Alex's kids. Alex was allowed to go through normal boarding process, however.

Since I was a US citizen and did not have multi-visit visa, they took my passport and my luggage and told me to follow the officers. I followed the armed officer who escorted me to a van, with three additional armed officers with automatic weapons in their possession. The officer kept my passport and my luggage and asked me to get in the van. They told me they would drive me directly to the plane and give my passport and luggage to the

Ukrainian flight attendant, who would return it to me once I was on Ukrainian soil. It was March and snowing outside, wet snow. It was cold, it looked gray and as we drove on the tarmac, I got very nervous with their stern looks and what seem like a very long road ahead. I had read many books and seen many movies so I had some idea what the KGB was capable of doing and how I could've very easily disappeared, and no one would've known what had happened to me. Maybe it was just my overactive imagination, but in my head, that felt like a possibility.

We kept driving and driving and soon they turned toward an airplane and as we got closer, I saw that it was a Ukrainian airline and there was a flight attendant who waved at them from the top of the stairs. I felt slightly relieved that they did not have plans to take me to Siberia. As we got to the plane, they escorted me out and walked up the stairs with me, gave my passport and luggage to the flight attendant with instructions and left. She seemed very pleasant, with kind eyes and a warm smile and as she escorted me to my seat, she told me not to worry and that I would get my passport and luggage when we land in Dnepropetrovsk. I noticed that there was no one else on the plane except me. I just sat there, wondering what was going to happen next. Were they going to just fly me by myself? Was Alex going to be on this flight? Would my visa situation have any implications on him since he was traveling with me? What was happening?

After about fifteen minutes or so, which felt much longer than that, I saw a passenger bus drive up to the plane and people got off the bus and onto the plane. I kept looking to see if Alex was one of them and once I saw him, I was relieved and felt more comfortable that at least he was going to be with me. I told him what had happened, as they had not provided him any details.

They had just told him that they were taking me to the plane and of course he felt angry for me and comforted me, apologizing for my experience. I was just glad I was safe and alive, although still wondering what to expect once we got to Ukraine.

Right before landing, the flight attendant came up to me and gave me back my passport and told me she would have my luggage by the exit door. I thanked her for her kindness. As we got out of the plane and started walking toward the building, I slipped and fell in the wet, cold, slushy snow. My pants were all wet and I thought, *this is not my day.* It had been a long day, I was tired and emotional, I looked wet and disheveled and this was the first time I was going to meet Alex's sister's family.

We had a few nice days in Ukraine, visiting with family and site-seeing and when it was time to return, we got on our rebooked flight from Dnepropetrovsk to Moscow and from there I continued on my original flight to Los Angeles. Once we got to Moscow, Alex and I said our goodbyes, which were always long and difficult. He walked toward the exit to go pick up his luggage and go home and I walked toward the transfer side to get to my next flight.

Going through customs, once again they stopped me and told me there was a problem with my ticket and they did not see any booking for me from Moscow to Los Angeles. I couldn't believe this was happening to me. What could be the problem now? I knew I had the ticket. They pulled me into an office, started questioning me once again and it was taking a very long time and I got very nervous that I would miss my flight. I expressed my concern to them, and they just ignored me and had conversation among themselves, being suspicious of me. What were they thinking? I was a spy? I showed them my confirmation, explained to them what had happened in terms of having to change my flight to

Ukraine because of a mistake in the visa and after some further discussion and exploration on their computer, they told me that my flight to Los Angeles was canceled because the original leg from Moscow to Ukraine was canceled and since it was all part of the same reservation, the entire remaining trip was canceled. By this time, I had already missed my flight and felt very frustrated. I asked them, "Can I please purchase another ticket?

She said, "No, we don't sell tickets here."

"Where can I purchase tickets from?"

"From the ticketing agency downstairs."

"OK, how can I get there to purchase new tickets?"

"You can't."

"Why not?"

"Because you would have to exit the customs and since you don't have a visa, you can't exit the customs area."

"What am I supposed to do? How can I get a flight back to Los Angeles?"

"I don't know, we have to wait for our manager to see what can be done. You may have to go back to Ukraine."

"Do you have a computer I can use to book another flight?

She replied, "No."

I was at my wits end at this point. I called Alex, who was already on the train going home and told him what had happened. I asked him if he could go to the ticketing office once he got off and book me another flight which he agreed to do, but he was not going to get there for another 45 minutes. He was very upset and wanted to return but I told him there was nothing he could do so there was no point in returning. Then I thought of my phone and tried to go online on my phone to rebook another flight. There was no Wi-Fi. I had to use my cell service, which was very slow, and I wasn't able to move through so I decided to call Travelocity to see if they could help me. With very little battery life left in my phone, I was able to book a flight from Moscow through New York to Los Angeles, leaving the same evening at an exorbitant price at the last minute and I knew my phone call would be very expensive too. But I did not care, I just wanted to get home, be on American soil and feel safe. Once I was able to book it, after a little while, the person at the counter was able to see my new booking online and they escorted me back through the immigration and customs area for me to get to my terminal and on to my flight.

In the meantime, I called Alex and told him not to book me another ticket, just in time as he was at the ticketing office already. I didn't even know how he would be able to book a last-minute ticket, as he did not have that kind of disposable money.

Once I got to New York, I felt much safer and reflected back on how inhumane, unfriendly and unhelpful all those immigration and customs agents I had interacted with in Moscow had been, and I never wanted to go back. It was not an experience I would forget. I at least had lived in the Soviet Union, understood Russian and knew some of their ways and how they would treat people. How about if it was an American or any other nationality who did not speak Russian, was not used to that type of treatment or was not aware of it? What a horrible experience for anyone to have.

I got back to Los Angeles and back to waiting for Alex's visa to get approved. In the meantime, we continued to write or Skype almost every day, sharing our days and at times, it was hard to believe how our feelings had resurrected, like a sleeping volcano, even stronger than before.

One day in June of 2012, I was in San Francisco for a business meeting and after work I had met Kyle and a couple of his friends for a Brazilian BBQ dinner. Whenever I was able to, I tried to see him when I was in San Francisco for work if our schedules allowed us, as it was not always so easy since he also had school and work. His grades had gradually improved, and I was happy to see him mature and become more responsible. I always enjoyed seeing him and having our deep conversations. Seeing him in person gave me a better sense of how he was doing overall.

After dinner, I decided to walk back even though it was a long walk. I thought I could speak with Alex on the phone at the same time and get some steps since I had been sitting in meetings all day and just had had a big dinner. We had a nice conversation, it was morning in Moscow and he was having his coffee and getting ready to go to work. We talked for about 20 minutes or so, and toward the end of the conversation, he started sounding a little different like he was really tired and not as engaged or wanted to get off the phone. I thought maybe he was in a hurry because he had to leave for work. We said our goodbyes and I told him that I would write to him as soon as I got to the hotel so he could have my email by the time he got to the office.

I did write him and waited to see if he was going to be online so we could chat after he got my email but he never came on. It got very late and I needed to go to sleep as I had an early meeting the next morning. When I got up the next morning, the first thing I did was check to see if there was a response but there wasn't. I thought maybe he got very busy at work and had to leave the office, which his work often required and thought I would check later in the evening for a response. That evening, when I got home, I checked for a response again and still nothing. I started worrying and called him, but he did not answer. This went on for few days. I got really concerned and did not know what to do or whom to call to find out if he was OK. Then he finally called me and I asked very worried if he was OK. He told me he had had another heart attack and he was at the hospital and would stay there for a couple of weeks as they needed to do some tests and he needed to recover.

I wasn't sure how things worked at the hospitals in Moscow, but two weeks sounded like a really long time and I was worried that it might be very serious, but it was hard to tell being so far away. Based on his description of how they were treating him and how some equipment was not working and they had to wait until it was fixed, it seemed to me that he was not necessarily getting the best care or even the care he truly needed. His children lived in Tambov with their mother and grandmother, which was about 285 miles away, his brother lived over two hours away, and his sisters lived in Armenia and Ukraine. Knowing that he had no immediate family close by, I was concerned that he was all by himself and no one was there to support him and to advocate for him or look out for his interests to make sure he was getting the treatment he needed. I had been through so many surgeries and hospitalizations with my parents and I knew how important it was to have a family member by your side.

A few days later he told me that his sister from Armenia was going to come and stay with him and look after him. I was happy to hear that and at the same time I thought that it must be serious if she is coming. Even when he got home, he would have a long recovery time. It was so hard to be so far away and not have a good sense of what was happening and how bad his situation was; but from what I could tell from our conversations, it sound quite serious, although he downplayed the situation and did not want me to worry. Given the status of his health, I was not sure about what the future held for us and he kept reassuring me that he would get better and telling me not to worry.

I did not share any of this with family or friends. I knew what they would say. Once again, they would question my judgment and discourage me from going through with my decision. I did speak with the sister who was there and wanted to hear from her that he was getting better, he was getting strong, and he was going to be OK. She reassured me that she would make sure he did.

By July he was better and back to work and his sister had returned to Yerevan. I was relieved and yet worried, not knowing for sure if he got the proper care and when this might happen again and whether he would survive the next heart attack. We still did not know how much longer it was going to take for him to get approval for his visa and we decided to meet again in Dubrovnik for a week. I was hesitant to go to Moscow based on my last experience and wondered if I was in their system now as someone who tried to get into the country without the proper visa. However, I also wanted to see Alex with my own eyes, be around him so I could get a better sense of his health. It got harder and harder to wait and our time in Dubrovnik was much needed.

We were so happy to see each other and spend a week in Croatia. I was relieved to see him strong and in good spirits; he looked better than before. He had gotten his teeth fixed, smoked and drank less and he had gained some weight which he was good for him. His sister had taken really good care of him by cooking for him and helping him recover and I was very happy to see the positive results.

We really enjoyed our time in Dubrovnik and when we were both parting to go back to our respective countries, we hoped that this was the last time we would meeting like this and next time we would meet in Los Angeles. He hoped he would be in Los Angeles by October 7th, which was the date that our love connection had truly started, when we ran into each other on my way to the post office in 1979. Now it was almost 33 years later and it looked like once again we would be together. Was that even possible? What were the chances that something like this could happen in life? We both felt very blessed and grateful and acknowledged not many had the privilege of experiencing this type of love and friendship. It was truly a gift and for us, an opportunity to love and be loved once again, the way we both craved. We talked and dreamed about how life was going to be for us when we finally were together and at times, it did not feel real, it felt like a fantasy, a movie, a book, not something that just happens to ordinary people. He always wanted to and talked about one day writing a book about our love and for that, he wanted to live on an island or somewhere in the mountains in a little cabin, away from everyone and only with me. In his diary, which I still have today, he described this desire even in his youth, after we were apart and had not yet re-connected.

Reuniting with Alex after 32 Years

O ctober 7th came and passed, but Alex still did not have his approval, although they had scheduled an in-person interview with him. He was disappointed that he could not be here by October 7th and a little concerned that they did not say anything after the interview as to when he could expect to get the visa or if anything else was still missing. However, his anxiousness did not last too long. Shortly after the interview, he got a letter and by mid-October, he had his visa for 90 days. He called me, ecstatic. We were both very excited that after such a long process, he finally had his approval and would be coming to the US. I remember driving home with a friend one evening after dinner and sharing with her that Alex was coming the following week. I explained the process and told her how we needed to get married within 90 days after he came so he did not lose his visa and could stay. She said, "How well do you really know him as an adult? He is coming here with nothing; have you thought about a pre-nuptial agreement before you marry him? You need to protect yourself, your son and all you have worked for."

I said, "He is leaving his job and his children and moving here to be with me, for love. If I am not sure about this after having gone through all we have gone through, then I have no business marrying him. If I need a pre-nuptial agreement, then there is no trust and how do you start a relationship with no trust? If I am wrong, then I will have to deal with it but true love is worth taking the risk for. Money can buy a wife or a girlfriend, but not love. You can always make money, it's a renewable resource."

I don't know if she agreed with me, but she accepted my response. I knew she came from a place of love. She had seen me go through a lot and wanted to protect me but in the end, she just wanted me to be happy.

Alex flew to Los Angeles on October 20th, and I went to the airport to pick him up. He specifically told me that he didn't want anyone at the airport except me. After all, we had waited a very long time for this moment, and he wanted that moment to be ours. In the meantime, my family was already at my house waiting to meet him. We had a family BBQ to celebrate and he got to meet everyone. Despite my family's hesitations about my choice, they were very gracious, just like they always had been in the past with my not-so-popular choices.

We went to Santa Barbara on October 22nd and got married at Santa Barbara courthouse the morning of October 23rd. We did not want to go anywhere for a honeymoon, thinking we could always go somewhere later as we wanted to make sure that we had the paperwork in motion to start his citizenship process. The law was that we had to get married within 90 days, otherwise his visa would expire and once we got married, he could apply for a green card, which he did the same week.

Less than a week later, he experienced his first Halloween, and in November, Alex had his first Thanksgiving. It was a particularly special one since it fell on his 50th birthday. This was truly a Thanksgiving to be grateful for many things for both of us and for rediscovering our love and finally being together after 32 years. He also had his first American Christmas and New Year's and enjoyed the holiday season, which was celebrated a little differently than what he was used to.

About five months after he applied for a green card, we had an interview with the immigration officer and after a thorough interview with some very intimate questions to validate our marriage that made us both feel very awkward, he got approved to get his green card which he received a few weeks after the interview.

This was a new life for him, starting everything from the beginning from a social security card to language classes, to driving lessons to get a driver's license, to going on job interviews and just learning about the country and life in America. Alex had never driven in his life since he didn't have the need to. Everywhere he lived, there was adequate public transportation. This was a new life for me too—helping him through the process, introducing him to friends and family and teaching him about the country. He had become a great companion to my mom while he was home during the day and they enjoyed their daily coffee together and watched *The Price is Right* together. She also took the opportunity to teach him about the everyday customs in the US and she enjoyed his company and their conversations.

We would walk in the evenings together after dinner and I started to notice that Alex couldn't keep up with me and had to stop often to catch his breath. I knew it was his heart and I knew he was taking medication and knowing his past history, I scheduled an appointment for a physical for him in addition to an eye exam and dental exam just so we could assess what his healthcare needs were. After his visit to our family primary care physician, he was referred to a cardiologist. As I expected, the doctor could tell from the medications he was taking and the physical exam that his heart needed attention. We did follow up with a cardiologist and after the initial exam, he ordered some follow up tests.

In the meantime, he went on job interviews and was anxious to start working. We decided that we should take a quick vacation, as it may be a while before he could take time off if he started a new job and especially since we didn't have a honeymoon when we got married. We decided it would be nice to go to Hawaii as Hawaii was considered paradise for anyone from Europe or faraway places. He couldn't believe that he was actually going to be in Hawaii. When you lived in Russia, you saw Hawaii on TV, you heard about it, you dreamt about it, but you didn't actually ever think you might one day be there. He enjoyed and admired the beauty of Hawaii but even in Hawaii, he had a hard time swimming and he felt chest pains.

Once we came back, he went for the follow up tests and we met with the cardiologist again. We learned that his heart was in pretty bad shape, his heart capacity was at 15-20% and they needed to schedule an angiogram and depending how it looked, they may be able to put a stent in. The cardiologist encouraged us to schedule the angiogram as soon as possible as he was concerned that if Alex had another heart attack, he may not have been able to survive it. He was the same cardiologist that my mom had been seeing and he was also head of cardiology for the hospital where Alex would have his angiogram. I trusted him and we scheduled the angiogram for the first available date, which was a few days after the appointment.

Losing Alex

The day before Alex was scheduled for his angiogram, my mom had an AFib, which was not the first time, but this time Alex was the only one home with her. Alex panicked and my mom had told him not to call me because I was already worried about the procedure he was going to have the next day and she asked him to call my older sister. When he called my sister, she told him to call 911 and she would be on her way. When the ambulance came, they took her to the hospital and Alex was worried about her. When I got home that day, I was surprised my mom was not in the family room watching TV and I asked Alex where she was and it was only then when he told me what had happened and explained why he hadn't called me to tell me. After I spoke with my sister and found out where my mom was, we got in my car right away and went to the hospital. When we got there, she was in stable condition and they were going to keep her overnight to do some further tests before they released her the next day or the day after.

The next morning, Alex and I went to the hospital, a different one than the one my mom was at for his angiogram. As I waited for the procedure to be over, I was nervous but at the same time, I was thankful that he was in this country and could get proper care and we were able to do what was needed before he had another incident. I was also optimistic that everything was going to be OK. After all, both my parents had had bypass surgeries and they lived over 20 years after that. This was fixable. After what felt like a long time, the doctor came out to speak with me and told me that he had several arteries that were blocked and one of them was the left main artery (widow maker) and he needed an urgent triple bypass. They scheduled the surgery the same evening.

My mom was still in the hospital and one of my sisters was with her and my other sister came to be with me. Everything was happening so fast, we had not even had a chance to let his family know and I was uneasy about it but at the same time, I didn't want them to worry. I was worried about both Alex and my mom as my mom had been frail and I had just found out that Alex's heart was in pretty bad shape. As worried as I was, I was trying to be strong and think positive but at the same time I could not help but think that things could go wrong. Knowing how weak his heart was, I wondered how well he could handle the surgery. Knowing how long he had smoked and drank excessively, I wondered what other health issues he may have that we had not discovered yet.

As my sister and I were waiting for the doctor to come out, I saw Marcelo's mother, Gloria come out of the elevator. She approached us and I asked her why she was at the hospital and she told me that Marcelo's father Frank, who I was fond of, was in the hospital and was not doing well. He was connected to life support and he did not have much more time to live. I knew he had had several health issues recently, was hospitalized a couple of months ago and I had even visited him at the hospital; but I did not realize he had deteriorated so quickly after that. When I had seen him at the hospital a couple of months ago, Gloria was there too, and I had told them that I had gotten remarried and they congratulated me. Frank squeezed my hand and gave me a hug and a kiss. I could tell he was genuinely happy for me. Gloria did not seem to be too happy about it. Now, I did not want to tell Gloria I was there for Alex and she did not ask. Later I had found out that she had assumed we were there for my brother-in-law for some reason. She looked sad and tired and left quickly. I was very tempted to go upstairs and see Frank, not knowing how much longer he had to live, but I did not want to miss the doctor when he came out after finishing Alex's surgery. I also did not want to run into Marcelo, especially at a time like this. I thought since Frank was in the same hospital, I could stop by during the day in the next couple of days.

The surgery took longer than expected and I wondered if there were further complications and why it was taking so long. Finally, the doctor came out and told us that the surgery went as well as expected. He indicated that the next 24 hours were critical. Alex was in Cardiac Intensive Care Unit and I could see him for a few minutes, but he was not awake. The doctor said I should just go home and come back the next morning. I did go see him and I was relieved he had survived the surgery and I believed that once he was past the initial 24 hours with no complications, he would be OK and we would just need to focus on recovery. His eyes were closed, and he looked as bad as you would expect after a major surgery. I was thankful that we were able to get him the help he needed in time. I went home exhausted, both physically and emotionally and tried to get some sleep before I returned the next morning.

The next morning Alex was still in Cardiac ICU but he was awake and even smiled when he saw me. He was able to sit up in his bed in the morning and later that day he was even able to stand up. I had called and informed one of his sisters about the surgery and that he was in recovery and had asked her to let the rest of the family and his children know. They were all very concerned and wanted to know how he was after the surgery, so I called his children and let them know that the surgery had gone well and he was recovering. He wanted to speak with his children so I brought my iPad so we could Skype with them. He was in good spirits when he spoke with them in the evening and he was looking forward to starting his recovery and cardiac rehabilitation once he was discharged. The doctor wanted to keep him in Cardiac ICU one more night before they moved him to a regular bed. That evening, my spirits were up too. I felt like the worst was over and now we just had to stay positive and work on his rehabilitation. My mom had come home too and when I got home, we had a light dinner together and as I had a glass of wine, I told my mom, "I feel so happy. I have not felt this happy for a long time, but I am almost afraid to feel this happy because I don't want anything bad to happen anymore."

She smiled and said, "Don't be afraid, everything is going to be fine."

The next day I was back at the hospital and they had moved Alex to a regular bed. He was able to sit and eat, he felt stronger, and he was starting his breathing exercises. The therapist walked him a few steps to the bathroom and I was glad he was doing so well. He even had some visitors. While I was at the hospital that day, I got a call from a friend who told me Frank had passed away. I was sad to hear the news, but he had been suffering for a while and I knew he was at peace now. I had tried to go see him one more time the day before, but when I had walked up to his room, I had heard Marcelo's voice and turned around and never entered his room. I was sorry I never got to say goodbye to him in person, but I was glad I had seen him a few weeks before.

The following day, Alex did even more in terms of walking and breathing exercise and his cousins came to visit and they were surprised at how well he was doing. He smiled and joked with them and started to get excited about being discharged in a day or two. This was Saturday evening and we were told that if he continued to do well Sunday and Monday, he would probably get discharged on Tuesday. They gave me discharge instructions so I could prepare for it, purchasing the things we needed for cleaning his scar on his chest, pain medication and making any arrangements for cardiac rehabilitation. He hadn't gone to the bathroom yet and felt discomfort in the evening, so they gave him something to loosen his stool to help him go to the bathroom. He wanted me to leave, as he felt uncomfortable going to the bathroom in his condition while I was there. I respected his wishes and frankly I was exhausted and wanted to get some rest. I left late at night to go home, and on my way home stopped and got a few things from the pharmacy and went to sleep with a smile on my face ready to go back in the morning and find him even stronger.

The next morning, before my alarm went off, my house phone rang and as I answered it, I realized that it was the hospital and I was immediately concerned. Why would they call me, especially this early and on my house phone? As the woman on the other end of the line started talking, I couldn't even understand what she was saying, I could just tell from her voice that something was wrong with Alex. I hung up the phone, put some clothes on and drove to the hospital.

Once I got there, I parked my car and ran inside the hospital toward Alex's room, but his room was taped with a note not to enter. I first thought maybe he got some type of infection that he needed to be isolated. As I ran toward the nurse's station, one of the nurses came up to me and said the doctor needed to speak with me. I said, "What's wrong? Why is my husband's room taped up? Where is he?"

At that moment, one of the ER doctors walked up to me, as he had been on duty that night and told me, "Alex had some challenges early this morning. He went into cardiac arrest and we could not save him. His heart was not strong enough yet to sustain the arrest and it may have been a clot, but we won't know for sure until we do the autopsy."

I felt weak. My knees buckled and I thought I was going to pass out when one of the nurses held me and another one got a chair for me to sit on and gave me some water. I couldn't believe this was happening to me again. I said, "But he was doing so well. He was here, at the hospital. What do you mean you couldn't save him? You have everything you need here at the hospital to save people. Was he being monitored? Were the nurses paying attention? Where is the nurse who was on duty? I need to speak with her to understand exactly what happened."

They told me her shift was over at 7:00 a.m. and she had gone home. I just could not believe it and got emotional. They were trying to comfort me, and I was in a daze; it did not feel real. Once I was able to breathe again, they asked me if I wanted to spend a few minutes with him before they sent him to the morgue. I was so weak, I could barely stand or walk and one of the nurses walked with me to his room, pulled a chair next to his bed and told me she would give me some private time with him.

I touched his face, which looked very peaceful and was still warm, but he was not there. I kissed his forehead. I held his hand and hugged him but there was no response. I spoke to him; I spoke to God in vain. This all looked so familiar, new wound on top of an old wound, just bleeding my heart. It was unreal. I wasn't sure if I was awake or in my sleep. *Where do I go from here?*

After spending some time with Alex, in my thoughts and in disbelief, I told them I was ready to leave. What else could I do? I looked for my phone and realized that I had left it at home when I left in a hurry, still connected to charge as I did every night. I couldn't remember anyone's number, but then realized Alex's cell phone was in the room and he had my sisters' numbers in his phone. I called one sister and told her Alex is gone.

She said, "What do you mean, I thought he was doing so well?"

I said, "He was, but he is gone, just gone," and started crying, and my sister was crying too. They gave me his stuff in a bag, just like they had done with Richard. I had just turned 50 less than a month ago. We had gone out to a Russian restaurant with my family and I had danced my heart out and so did Alex. I had finally found love again and was content, even with all the challenges. This was not supposed to happen. As I got home, my mom asked me how Alex was. She had just assumed I had left to go to the hospital to visit him. She was still asleep when I left in the morning and no one had told her yet. I told her Alex was gone and she asked, "How?"

I said, "Gone, like Richard."

She said, "How? What do you mean?" She could not comprehend and once she realized, she started crying and screaming and her heart was palpitating and I was worried that she was going to have another AFib only a few days after her last one and she wouldn't survive. We couldn't have this happening and thankfully my sisters were there and they calmed her down and gave her water. I was just so emotionally drained and exhausted, I could not even think and most of what was being said I could not hear. I just knew there was a lot of commotion and I wanted to take a hot shower, crawl into my bed and be alone.

The next few days were a blur to me: people visiting, arrangements being made, and phone calls with his family and his sisters, which were very difficult and heart-wrenching. They had a lot of questions and I did not have many answers. Although they knew he had had a heart condition, I didn't think they realized how damaged his heart was. Part of me felt responsible for taking their father, their brother away from them and now he was gone. I felt guilty that no one from his family was here and they were not able to get visas and travel to be here even for his funeral. I felt responsible that he was in the US because of me and that this happened while he was with me, barely just starting our life together. I questioned our decision about the surgery and wondered if he would have had a little longer time to live, even with his sick heart, had we not done the surgery. His life was in danger with the heart he had, and his damaged hart was not going to allow him to continue to live. We had talked about his health before he had moved to the US and he had said that even if he only had one year to live, he wanted to be with me and he wanted to take that chance. He was in the US for only seven months, which was the same amount of time we had together before I moved to the US in 1980.

My son said, "Mom, you gave a dying man his last wish. That's love. Not many people would have done that."

I really believed that with access to better healthcare, we could've fixed the damage to his heart and he would have had a chance to have a longer and healthier life. Why do people with heart of gold also have very sick hearts? Richard and Alex both had beautiful, loving, kind, giving and generous hearts yet we lost them both because of their sick hearts. Why did some people who drink and smoke all their lives and are not good people get to live for a very long time? The world needs more kind and loving people, yet sometimes we lose them too soon.

I was in that same space I had been when Richard had passed away—questioning my faith, asking many questions—yet I knew that sometimes there are just no answers, no logical explanations. How was I going to reconcile this in my mind, in my heart and what lasting effect was this going to leave on me, on his children, on his family and on my faith in love, belief in fairness, in goodness and in hope?

Alex really had wanted to be cremated. We had talked about it for some reason and when he found out I wanted to be cremated, he expressed a desire to be cremated as well so that our ashes could join one day again. Once we had the autopsy results, which confirmed that he did not have a clot and there was nothing more they were able to find that caused his death other than his heart was not strong enough to handle the cardiac arrest, I started making arrangements. When I brought up his wishes regarding cremation to his sisters, one of his sisters felt strongly that he should be buried and not cremated, that cremation was not accepted by their faith and beliefs. Considering how hard this was for them, being so far away and not having had the opportunity to truly discuss this in person, I followed their wishes, as I did not want to create any ill feelings. I felt guilty enough for what had happened and at the same time, I felt very responsible for doing the right thing, as I was the only person here with him having to make these types of decisions and arrangements. I did apologize to Alex in my heart and in my mind and hoped that he would understand and forgive me.

I was all too familiar with the cemetery, with the funeral arrangement process, with the service in the chapel and even the pastor who I had used for Richard, for my father and now for Alex. Pastor Bruce did a beautiful service and we had a meal to celebrate his very short-lived life and remembered him for the seven months he was with us. As it always goes with those things, everyone goes home and moves on with their lives, just as I would have to do at some point, as life does not stop for anyone's grief. I went back to work after a couple of weeks, back to my routine, going through the motions, living like a robot and contemplating what was next for me and how to move from my deep sadness to a more "life is worth living" state.

What More Can Happen?

I tried to engross myself in work and shift my focus from my grief to challenges at work. Weeks were going by and life was moving forward and I still had a hard time smiling or feeling joy in anything. I had gotten promoted a few months before Alex passed away and had to lay off some people and reorganize my entire team and re-align to execute on our strategy and meet some very challenging goals set forth for us. I was feeling the pressure. At times, it was difficult to focus at work and keep my energy high and be an enthusiastic leader. I did not want my grief to reflect on my job and I did not want to let my team down. I often worked late or traveled and felt physically and emotionally exhausted. As much as I loved my job, I had a hard time finding meaning in it. I would come home and eat something light, have a glass of wine and either go for a walk or listen to music. My family was frustrated with me as I was not in the mood to talk when they came over. I didn't want to do much or go anywhere. I was sad and still kind of in a haze. My mom tried to get me to watch TV with her or she'd tell me about whom she spoke to when she went for her daily walks in the morning or what she had heard in the news, but I just could not engage and she really did not like that. She complained to my sisters that I did not want to talk to her. She kept saying it should have been her because she was much older and Alex had his life ahead of him but who is to decide? I just did not want to hear any of it. There was nothing we could do any more and I found myself having to comfort her and tell her that it was not her time and I was glad she was here and still with us.

Less than two months later, in August of the same year, it was early morning and I had just gotten out of the shower and was getting ready for work, I got a call from my mom. She had been out walking in the morning, as she did every day in our neighborhood. I thought maybe she needed me to do something before I left for work, but she told me she had fallen on the street and could not get up. I rushed to put some sweats on and went out there hoping that she was OK. As I got there, she was on the ground and she was in a lot of pain and crying. I tried to help her, but she was in too much pain and I did not want to move her too much in case she had broken something. I called 911 and they came very quickly and after checking her briefly, they decided they needed to take her to the hospital. I came back to the house, got in my car while they were putting her in the ambulance and followed them.

My sisters and I had been frustrated that she was not using a walker or a cane to help as at times she got light-headed and would lose her balance. She had fallen a few times at home but fortunately she hadn't broken anything. We were concerned that the next time she fell, she would break something and now it had happened. Once she got to the hospital, they took some x-rays and did tests and determined that she had a break in the upper part of her femur close to her hip and needed surgery.

The surgery went well, however, given her age, the recovery was not going to be so easy. She was in the hospital for few days and then she was in a rehabilitation center for a while. When she was released to go home, she needed physical therapy. Unfortunately, I did not have a bedroom downstairs, so she had to stay with my sister who had a one-story house.

I was still dealing with my loss and at the same time trying to manage my demanding job with frequent out of town travel, having to visit her at the hospital, then at the rehab center and later at my sister's house and worrying about her recovery, which was all very stressful. I had our dog Peaches whom I was leaving alone all day and I needed to get home to feed him and check on him. My mom wanted to move back to my house as that was her home but the only way she could do that was by being able to go up and down the stairs again. After some time, her physical therapist also came to my house with her to help her learn how to properly go up and down the stairs. She was a good patient in terms of doing her therapy and she had the will to want to walk again, drive again, and go up and down and stairs so she could return home. She was able to accomplish that almost two months later.

When my mom returned home, it eased the schedule and it was nice for Peaches not to be alone all day. My mom was doing really well and becoming more independent and starting to drive again which made her happy and gave her the freedom back to see her friends, to go to the senior center, to do whatever she wanted to do.

One day I came home, and she told me that Peaches had not eaten all day and she did not want to get up. When I walked in, Peaches looked weak and sad and I looked on the side of the house where we had the dog run and where she normally went to relieve herself and noticed that her urine was bloody. I couldn't believe that now that my mom was finally home and she was doing well, Peaches was having health issues. I did not know what it was and wasn't sure what it was going to involve but I knew I needed to take her to the veterinarian. I tried to see if she would get up to go for a walk or to get a treat and although she tried, she did not stay up very long. I knew how much she loved her treats and going for a walk and when she couldn't even do that, I knew something was seriously wrong with her.

I took her to the veterinarian. They kept her overnight to do some tests and when I went back the next day, I was told that she had kidney failure. I didn't even know dogs could get kidney failure. The next few days were challenging as she would not eat, she had some water but bloody urine and she could barely get up and there was no chance of her getting better. She was suffering and there was nothing more we could do. I decided it was time to put her to sleep. Although I was with her, my son was upset that he could not be with her. Peaches was Kyle's dog and we got her for him when he turned ten so he really loved her. He wanted me to wait until Christmas but Peaches could not last that long and I did not want her to die while I was at work or at night by herself. I tried to comfort him and told him that he could not miss his finals to fly home for this and he could just be with Peaches in spirit. It was just before Christmas and he was going to be home in less than two weeks. However, he still wished he could be with her and was not very happy with my decision. After all, this was his dog. We got Peaches when she was only seven months old and she was with us for almost fifteen years and she had become a family member. We had yet another loss in the same year. What else could go wrong? It was another sad Christmas and I just could not see myself being home for New Year's since that was my favorite holiday, and the year before I had been in Moscow with Alex.

Digging Deep for Strength

A couple of months before the end of the year, I had already been thinking that I wanted to be away for New Year's; maybe I could go on a trip. I remembered how my Machu Picchu trip had helped me as part of my healing process when Richard had passed away, and how much I had enjoyed Kyle's company. I asked him if he would be interested in going on a trip with me over his winter break and he was very open to it. He loved traveling and we traveled well together. Whether it was The Great Wall in China, Ayers Rock in Australia, Table Mountain in South Africa, Sugar Loaf in Brazil or just site-seeing in Europe, Kyle had always been an amazing travel partner. I so enjoyed seeing things through his viewpoint.

I wanted to do something we hadn't done before and initially, we talked about going to Antarctica since that was the only continent we had not been to. After we explored that option, it was going to be too expensive, considering how late we were going to book so we decided not to go to Antarctica. As it turned out, later on the news, we found out that the vessel we were going to go on had gotten stuck there. A Russian ice cutting vessel had to go rescue them and they were stranded for quite some time. A few days after our decision about Antarctica, when I was having lunch with my friend Gretchen, she told me about her Kilimanjaro trip, the 4th highest mountain in the world, and it sounded so adventurous and challenging. I said to her, "I would love to do that, but I imagine I would need to train to do that. I don't think I can do that in time to travel by the end of December."

She said, "You can absolutely do that. If I can do it, you certainly will have no problem doing it." Since she was in the travel business and knew all I was going through, she offered to help me plan for it. When I suggested it to Kyle, he was all excited about it and he was up for the challenge as always. He was doing better at school and making better choices but not always and still had some maturing to do. I thought it would be great to spend some quality time with him.

When I shared our decision to go to Kilimanjaro with my family and friends, some were very encouraging and supportive and had confidence we could do it and some felt we were crazy and questioned my judgment once again. They thought I had lost my mind and felt this was something drastic and high risk. They wondered why I would choose a trip like this when there were so many other places in the world to go. None of that made me change my mind and once I make up my mind, I am very likely to follow through with my goal.

Over the next few months, I started hiking more, alone, with any friend who wanted to hike and few times with Kyle when he visited. We couldn't train for the elevation, but we could at least train for endurance. I put weights in my backpack for the hikes; I found higher mountains that were not too far to drive to and hiked them; I used the Stairmaster at the gym and soon it was time to go. We also prepared by making sure we had the right hiking boots and all the right equipment to make sure those kinds of things were not going to get in the way of us reaching the peak. After all, I was not sure if we would have another opportunity to do this. We left a couple of days after Christmas to spend the New Years in Ngoro Ngoro crater and do a little mini safari before our Kilimanjaro hike. We spent the New Year at a farm and really enjoyed the people we met and the food they prepared for us with farm grown fruits and vegetables and farm-raised chicken and other things. After the farm, it was time for our Kilimanjaro hike through the Rongai route, which was believed to be the easiest, the driest, the quietest and the only route approaching from the north side of the mountain.

We met our group with G Adventures in Moshi, Tanzania the day before the hike, where we got the briefing and introduced ourselves and met others. There were twelve in our group and all were very friendly, were well-traveled and had great senses of humor. We had people from England, Scotland, Australia, Germany and Sweden. Kyle and I were the only Americans. Everyone was in their 20s or early 30s except the Scottish guy, who was 45 and had done the base camp at Everest. I was the oldest at 50 and Kyle was the youngest at 22. We had teachers, an IT guy, an economist, a doctor, a lawyer, an Army guy, a photographer and a product manager in our group. Our guides themselves were very young and they decided that since I was the oldest person in the group, they would call me "Mama," so the whole group called me mama the entire time.

The next morning, we started from the lush green belt with potato fields and coffee plantations, which eventually turned into pine forests and then alpine deserts all the way to the snow-covered peak of Kilimanjaro at 19,340 feet. The first night we were camping, we saw people being carried down from altitude sickness and other injuries. They looked young and in shape and I was nervous, but so far, the hike had not been too hard. The next couple of days, we saw a few more people being carried down.

On the fourth day, we reached the base camp, which was an interesting experience. There were groups from different parts of the world. The energy level was high and people were exchanging stories. Some were nervous, some were excited, some had done this hike several times and there were first timers like us.

Before we started our summit climb at 12:00 a.m. on the fifth day from the base camp, I said to Kyle, "If I get sick, I will come down, but you continue. If you get sick, we will both come down. I don't want to do this without you." Of course he argued about the fairness of my suggestion, but we decided to put off coming to an agreement until we had to make that decision.

Throughout our six-day hike we were very lucky to mostly have sunshine, but our trekking experience included dust, mud, crossing creeks, snow, ice and hail. All our guides, porters and cooks were very kind, warm, helpful and encouraging, and they worked very hard every day. They cooked for us, woke us up with a hot tea every morning in our tents, and on the last day, they did everything they could to make sure we reached the peak. As we started our midnight hike toward the peak, it quickly became very challenging hiking in the dark with only headlights, the cold, the wind, the light snow, the altitude and watching people at every few feet stop, return or throw up. We were going very slowly with the goal of reaching the top at sunrise. At some point, the straws for the water bottles were frozen and so were the camels. You would have to open the top of the bottle with the hope of getting a few drops and it was too cold to even stop for that. Once we got to Gillman's Peak, we knew we only had a couple more hours left but the hardest leg of the climb. By that time, we were surrounded with snow; it felt freezing cold even with six layers of clothing and even with our faces covered. Unfortunately, one of the teachers from Australia and the two German girls from our group only made it to Gillman's Peak, as they were too sick to continue. It was still a great accomplishment to reach Gillman's Peak.

The next two hours were treacherous. It was hard to breathe and the pace was very slow. It was truly going poli-poli (very slow). Once we got to the top of Uhuru Peak, it was -17C and windy. My camera and phone batteries froze within ten minutes. All that treachery was worth the amazing view at the top, including the glaciers. Even though I thought I was going to pass out from exhaustion and could no longer feel my fingers, I was exhilarated and couldn't stop crying at the same time. I couldn't believe we were on top of Kilimanjaro, watching the beautiful sunrise and most importantly, I was with my son. It was an emotional moment for me for many reasons in addition to being overwhelmed by the beauty and what we had just accomplished. I knew at that moment that all my guardian angels (and I had a few) were watching over us all along the way and had made this possible for us. That is when I remembered the word "Ubuntu" in Zulu, which translates to "I am because of you" and in a more philosophical sense, it means the belief in the universal bond of sharing that connects all humanity. I knew and felt at a spiritual level my connection to my son, to my family, to my friends, to all I have loved, had known and will get to know one day and to humanity with the strong desire to share this moment with all.

We were only at the top for about 15-20 minutes before we started descending because of the altitude. I was just in such a delirious state that it did not feel real; it felt like a dream, it felt like an out of this world experience. Once we got back to base camp, we rested the remaining day, had a special celebratory dinner, but no alcohol yet, and prepared for the longest day, with a seventeen-mile descent the next day all the way to the bottom of the mountain.

Although I had not cremated Alex, I had had a burning ceremony of some of his clothes with a friend in my backyard and brought some of the ashes with me, which I released after dinner in the beautiful hills of base camp that night. I could feel he was with me at that moment and I could almost feel his smile. I knew my father and Richard were with us as well as their energy surrounded us all along. Even though there was a chilling wind, I could feel gentle warmth all around me.

The next morning, as we headed down, it got warmer and easier to breathe, although going down for an entire day made it very painful for our knees. Once we got back to Moshi, we finally were able to take a hot shower after six days and it was the best shower I have ever had in my life. We had yet another celebratory dinner that night, this time including alcohol. We played some games with our group, acknowledged and expressed our appreciation for our guides, our porters and our cooks.

The next day, we were ready to leave Tanzania and get home. This was by far the most physically and mentally challenging trip I have ever done. It was a once in a lifetime adventure, rewarding in so many ways. It was extra special for me being with Kyle. I am glad we chose to do this trip and it certainly felt healing in some ways for me. I was thankful that neither Kyle nor I got sick and we didn't have to make any difficult decisions. I also enjoyed the quality time Kyle and I got to spend over six days, sharing our tent, hiking, eating, playing, taking pictures, enjoying the views and feeling grateful for having the opportunity to do something like this.

Once we returned home, we were excited to share our stories with our family and friends. At times, it was hard to believe that we had actually climbed Kilimanjaro. It felt unreal. Our friends and family were proud of us and were glad we had returned safely and some were surprised that we actually did it but I think it also gave people the chance to think that they too can do it if they really want to and set their mind to it. I encouraged everyone who expressed interest to do it, every chance I got and I am so glad Gretchen encouraged me to do it. To this day, that's probably one of my greatest physically-challenging accomplishments and my favorite because Kyle was with me.

Soon after we returned from Kilimanjaro, Kyle went back to San Francisco to start school and I returned to work and although I was still feeling my loss deeply, there was something different about it. Somehow, I knew I was going to be OK and just as before, life would move on and although it had only been seven months, it felt like I was at a better place and I no longer wondered how I was going to survive another loss. I had learned that the pain from loss never diminishes but your life around it grows so that the pain occupies a small place. I needed to once again refocus on what I had rather than what I had lost and make a conscious effort to be in the present moment, appreciate the present moment and what was around me and how my not-so-desirable experiences were helping me grow in ways that I would otherwise never have had the opportunity to. As Diane Specht wrote after losing her son:

> There are many tears in our broken heart that never reach our eyes...
>
> There is a grief that ages the face and hardens the heart, yet softens the spirit...
>
> A grief that casts shadows on the eyes yet broadens the mind...
>
> A grief that keeps the pain and has no words, but increases the understanding...
>
> There is a grief that breaks the heart and wounds the soul that lasts and lasts and can shatter in a minute, but will inspire for a lifetime...

I knew I needed to continue to grow as a person. I knew I had to think way beyond myself. Everyone had a story and I wanted my story to inspire others. I did not want to feel sorry for myself nor did I want others to feel sorry for me. Often people said to me, "You don't deserve this." And my response was, "No one does." I knew that I was fortunate in many ways that others were not, I believe there is balance in the universe, and I believe there is divine energy that is beyond our human comprehension and much bigger than us. I knew there was a reason and a purpose and I just had to carry it out as gracefully as I could. I was thankful for having been chosen for the road less traveled which in turn was a fuller life giving me the opportunity to live my best life, to embrace what was part of my life's journey and in return give back to the universe with my positive energy, faith, kindness, generosity of heart, passion, hope and love that has no limits.

A few months later, Alex's sister who lives in Ukraine told me that she wanted to be here for his death's one-year anniversary. I had mixed feelings about it initially. I felt that it might bring back some of the deeper pain and I would regress from my path of healing, but I also thought it would help with the healing. I knew she really needed to be here, be with me. I was the last connection to her brother. There weren't many people I could reminisce with about Alex since not many knew him well here, but I knew I could do that with her and that was always a healing process.

She did come and it was very nice to have her here, for her to see where her brother lived the last few months of his life and where he was buried. It was a bittersweet visit but it was very much worthwhile spending that time together, reliving some of what had happened in the past 32 years, reminiscing about the good times and some of the not so good times and overall, being grateful that Alex lived his last couple of years with love in his heart which was so important to him; it was his life.

After she left, I took another hiking trip in September in Cinque Terre, not as challenging, but a beautiful coastal hike. I traveled by myself and although I wished I could share it with someone I loved, it was actually good to be alone.

To Love at All Is to Be Vulnerable

L ife itself is very unreliable and sometimes it brings you down to your knees, but if you stand up and take one step and another, you will find love. Even when you let go of the person, you never let go of the love; love surrounds you and has no measure or limits.

It was another ordinary day at work. I walked to the kitchen to get a cup of coffee in the morning, just as every morning I was in the office. As I poured coffee into my cup and added some sugar, he walked into the coffee room and approached the sink to rinse his cup.

"Hi, how are you" he asked me, without looking at me while he rinsed his cup.

"I am OK," I said. I noticed he had a white porcelain cup, almost like an English teacup, which was unusual for a man getting a morning coffee. He noticed me staring at it with perplexed look.

He said, "I know, this looks silly and very feminine, but I have a warmer on my desk and the regular mugs are too big for it. I like to keep my coffee warm while I am sipping it."

I barely smiled and didn't comment on it. I just said, "Have a good day," and started walking out of the kitchen.

Then he said with concerned voice, "I am tired of seeing you so sad. I really miss your smile." I was surprised that he had noticed or that he was so observant.

I forced a faint smile and responded barely looking at him, "It's a process. I'll get there, and I've done it before." Sometimes I wondered if I really could.

As I walked away, trying to avoid him noticing my tears, he said, "Sorry, that came out wrong. I can't even imagine what it's like."

"That's OK," I said as I walked away with my coffee, pondering the exchange we had. I had known him for many years, but never really had a conversation except maybe greetings. As I got to my desk, I remembered I had a small black cup that I did not use because it was too small, and I liked big mugs for coffee. I thought maybe I could offer it to him; it would look less "silly."

The next day, I messaged him offering the cup. He said he would love to have it and came by my office to pick it up. A few days later, I ran into him and asked him how the black cup was working out and he said it was fine and joked that most importantly it looked manlier. Then he said, "You are a skancheli person." The word in Armenian means "wonderful/beautiful."

I asked him how he knew that word and he said he had asked an Armenian friend how to say it so he could say it to me. I walked away smiling. A few days went by and I had not seen him. Then one day, he messaged me: "I'd like to thank you for the mug in person. Would you be open to having a drink with me?"

I said, "That would be nice."

Later that day when I ran into him in the hallway and as I glanced toward him for a moment, I saw him smiling. His eye lingering with warmth and an indefinable something else. My heart skipped a beat.

When we met for drinks the conversation flowed easily. We talked about our lives, about our mistakes and experiences and it felt like speaking with a long lost friend. He knew how to pour the right words into my soul just when I needed them the most. He knew how to hold my hand and not say anything and make me feel completely content as if he read my mind and knew I craved the magic of simplicity, watching the ocean waves and smelling the ocean, walking in the rain or gazing at the beautiful moon and the star-filled sky and enjoying 6 p.m. sunsets with colors that usually didn't belong in the sky.

After drinks, when he walked me to my car, he gave me a very faint kiss on the corner of my mouth and my cheek, without warning and without permission. I knew I would become homesick for that moment and I would long to be vulnerable in his arms. Maybe love comes to those who still hope, even though they have been disappointed, to those who still believe even though they've been betrayed, to those who still love, even though they've been hurt before.

How Will My Journey Evolve?

Kyle was living and working in the Bay Area and doing well, still evolving and still maturing and our interactions were now at a different level in a good way. It was enjoyable to see how family values were instilled in him, how much of what I thought he was not paying attention to when he was younger he actually was now repeating back and surprising me and how much of his father he had in him. He and I were going to attempt another New Year's trip together, this time to Cuba with my friends. I had to cancel the day before the trip because of a detached retina, but he felt comfortable enough to go with my friends and thoroughly enjoyed it. Michael was married and lived with his wife and two children in Virginia and still visited every so often. Although he did not keep in touch much and still felt very distant when he visited, he was working for my sister Annie's company and was very much still part of the family. I loved him and still hoped that one day he and Kyle would have a closer relationship. My mom still lived with me in the same house and she had more health challenges. Ironically, when I returned from one of my trips from Asia with a compound ankle fracture and fractured fibula, she had to take care of me.

Work had become my focus. Many changes happened at work in leadership, including my long-time boss leaving the company and me getting promoted to Senior VP with an even more demanding and stressful set of responsibilities. I was always proud of my team and what they were able to accomplish and throughout all the changes and challenges, we continued to succeed and deliver. Many people commented that my superpower was remaining calm and logical during most stressful situations and often asked me, "How do you stay so clam, how do you manage all this stress?"

I always thought to myself, *this is nothing compared to what I have already experienced in my life. What could be worse than losing two husbands, divorcing one, losing my father, my dog, climbing Kilimanjaro and raising a teenager as a single parent?* After all that, I was still here and I felt strong and I loved life and the experiences that came with it. The stress of work paled compared to that. I could handle anything. I felt powerful, confident, capable, and resilient. I was never concerned about the destination. Life's journey, including the challenges it came with both professionally and personally, was what helped me grow as a person continuously and overcoming those challenges gave me the most satisfaction. Everything that had happened to me was for me and I gracefully accepted it as a gift and as my path to who I was meant to be.

I lost my mother four years after Alex passed away, after being very ill for about two years and suffering from constant excruciating pain. I was glad she was able to attend Kyle's graduation with his BA in Biochemistry, even though she was in a wheelchair, and she lived to see him get his MS in Chemistry/ Material Science with summa cum laude and a research fellowship. She was proud of him, she loved him, and she was so happy to see him come such a long way from his first year of college, as she was always worried about him, probably even more than me. She had a special relationship with Kyle, having lived with us and she had developed this intimacy with him as they sent hand written letters to each other after Kyle moved to San Francisco. When he visited, they could talk about anything, and Kyle was always very open to her constructive feedback, even more so than to mine.

Somehow she was much less critical of his imperfections and choices than she was of mine. Maybe, as you get older you become more tolerant of mistakes and understand the importance of accepting people you love as they are. Her love had no limits for her grandchildren. As different as my mother and I were, we were also very similar in some ways and I see things in me today that remind me of my mother and I am thankful for it.

Her last two years were very challenging for her health-wise. She had compression fractures due to osteoporosis, which caused great pain in her back. There was not much they could do about it and the back brace they recommended was not comfortable to wear. She was already on several medications for high blood pressure, cholesterol, water retention and now pain. Being on several medications pushed her into vicious cycle of dealing with pain, then constipation, then diarrhea, then water retention, difficulty breathing, then dehydration and then the cycle would repeat. She was in and out of the hospital and at times, walked out with very strong opioid prescriptions. She had reached the same state as my father and she no longer wanted to live. Ironically, when my father first passed away, she wanted to continue living. She said, "Harry, I am not ready to go yet. I want to enjoy my children, my grandchildren, my great-grandchildren and life." But now, when she no longer had the will or desire to live, she said, "Harry, God doesn't love me, that's why he is not taking me. You don't love me either? Take me, I am ready now."

The pain and the constant discomfort along with her significant decline in quality of life had pushed her into a difficult mental state. Once again she had to move in with my sister for a while, then she was at a skilled nursing home with full time care and the last few days, hospice care at my sister Annie's house. She was able to be with her children and her grandchildren her last few days and die with dignity.

As difficult as it was to see my mother in such pain and discomfort for a very long time and as prepared as we were, it was not easy to accept that she no longer was with us. She was at a better place, or at least that's what I believed, and she was with my father and she could dance again with him.

About a year after my mother passed away, we had the Woolsey Fire and I had to evacuate. I was the only one living at the house at that time, a house that started with five residents and a dog only eighteen years ago. Fortunately, I did not lose my house, nor did I have much damage. I was able to return to my house after four days. Being away from my home and not knowing if my house was going to survive or not and wondering what I would do if lost my house forced me to really focus on not what I wanted to accomplish next, not professionally but rather who I wanted to be in the next phase of my life and when that next phase should start.

I no longer had any critical responsibilities except what I wanted to give back and pay forward. I did not want my life to be defined by my professional and material accomplishments. I wanted to live a life that mattered in my acts of service, generosity of heart, compassion and courage to enrich, empower, or encourage others. I decided to start thinking about leaving my corporate high-pressure executive position and start the journey for my second peak. I wanted to feed my soul by spending time on things I enjoyed and that were meaningful to me at this stage in my life. I wanted to spend my time, the most valuable and non-renewal resource we all have, doing all the things I always wanted to do but did not have the time for before, including: spending more time with people who meant the most to me, reading, listening to music, enjoying art, traveling, writing a book, serving and having time to reflect and contemplate and just be. Success is not measured by what we accumulate but by what we contribute, how we inspire others and serve where we are most needed. Most of my life, everything I had done had been for myself or my parents or my family or my son or my friends or my job and I wanted now to give back in a broader sense. I had been so fortunate and blessed to have had and experienced all that I had in my life and I felt very privileged. I felt a greater need to be part of the community, to be part of a "system" in serving and helping make a difference in a way that was meaningful to me, even if it was in just one person's life. It's gratifying to feed the homeless for the day, or volunteer at the food bank once in a while or clean the beach or work with Habitat for Humanity for a week or donate money for causes you believe in, but I wanted to choose and get involved in something that became part of my life long-term and in a more meaningful way to me. As Simon Sinek said, "When we help ourselves, we find moments of happiness. When we help others, we find lasting fulfillment."

After thinking and preparing myself for how I wanted to spend my time in this next phase of my life, I left my job less than a year after the fires to focus on renewing, recharging and rewiring my life. As they say, there is a job, there is a career and there is a calling and I wanted to embark on my calling. I felt liberated by my decisions. To start out, I got involved both with Big Sisters and CASA (Court Appointed Special Advocate), working with children who are in the system. My love for children and representing their interests, especially when their voice is often not being heard, has meaning for me. In addition, I started traveling more. Travel has always been a big part of my life and, as I once read, not to escape life but so that life does not escape me. What I enjoyed most was how travel made me feel inside and how it made me realize what an insignificant place we take in this world and there is so much more we can learn and experience in life. A friend once shared with me this quote by Pico Lyer: "If travel is like love, it is, in the end mostly because it's a heightened state of awareness, in which we are mindful, receptive, undimmed by the familiarity and ready to be transformed. That is why the best trips, like the best love affairs, never really end..."

I have traveled to over sixty countries and met many people who have inspired me by their kindness, humbleness, infinitely positive energy, generosity of heart and warm smiles even when they lived in the favellas of Brazil, the slums of India or suetos in Africa. I know that regardless of our circumstances, if we have an open heart, humility, hope and a desire to evolve to live our best lives, there will always be a rainbow and sunshine after the storm. I also learned that in life, as much as we aspire to be the perfect mother, perfect daughter, perfect sister, perfect employee, perfect friend, perfect partner, it's impossible to be. Some days we are at 100% and some days we are at much less than 100% and we have to allow ourselves to be human, embrace imperfection or we become increasingly insecure and hypocritical. What matters more is the intent and that comes from a place of love, deep down from our hearts and souls.

Epilogue

Sometimes the memories knock the wind out of me. I still cry when I hear certain songs or see something or eat something or smell something or read something or for no reason at all, or maybe for many reasons. It could be for Richard and how he loved me more than life itself. It could be for Alex who apologized for loving me and not forgetting me for over 30 years and for still wanting to be with me in his last months of life. It could be for Kyle who lost his father so young and to this day has the insatiable curiosity to learn more about his father and how he has become an amazing human being after all that he has been through. It could be for my father who loved me unconditionally and made me feel safe and confident, or my mother who always wanted what she thought was best for me and I always felt I came short of her expectations. And sometimes, it's for my story, even when it's more real than I wanted it to be but at the same time, rich in so many ways.

So maybe it's not about the happy ending, it's about the story. My story was not about broken dreams; my story was about a girl who could not be broken. Life does not have to be perfect to be wonderful. I read once that scars on you heart show that you have loved and scars on your body show that you have lived and I have both. You are never as broken as you think you are. Your heart is big enough to hold both sorrow and joy. The reality is that you will grieve forever. You will not "get over" the loss of loved ones; you will just learn to live with it. You will heal and you will rebuild yourself around the loss you have suffered. You will be whole again, but you will never be the same. Nor should you be the same, nor would you want to be the same. Letting go and moving on is hard and when you let go of the person you were with, you also have to let go of the person you were when you were with them. It's OK to be sad, it's OK to feel that the world around you is crumbling into million little pieces, it's OK to spend sleepless nights, it's OK to break down and cry and then cry some more, it's OK to feel completely vulnerable, and it's OK to feel lost, as long as you remember not to close the door that leads to your heart and have enough courage to love one more time.

Perhaps the most beautiful paradox of all is how human soul can be heartbreakingly fragile yet unbreakably strong at the same time. I didn't know what the future would bring, but I knew that there was more I wanted to experience, I wanted to continue feeding my wanderlust and I knew I wanted to die with memories, not dreams. I didn't want to live for some future goal. As they say, it's the side of the mountain that sustains life, not the top. I know that when the time is right, universe will continue to present me with opportunities.

Everyone has a story. I was just an ordinary immigrant girl who has had an extra-ordinary life journey and continue to do so. I wanted to write this book to inspire other women to share their stories and perhaps relate to moments in my life when I felt love or when I lost love, when I was betrayed and weak and made decisions out of fear, or when I was resilient and strong and stayed true to myself, when I made mistakes or I was in despair but found the courage to continue and another door opened up for me and I found love again. I have learned that love has no limits. Even when you lose love, if your heart is open to love, the universe will present you with opportunities to love again and again. There are people in this world who are unkind, mean, selfish, egotistic, violent, disrespectful, greedy and arrogant. There are people who lie and cheat and it's hard to love them, but even they need to be loved, as they are the ones who need love the most. Love is all around us, in different forms, and you have to be ready and have the capacity to receive it and give it. I know that true LOVE is worth living for and worth dying for.

Acknowledgements

I want to thank my editor and publisher Keidi Keating for her guidance, support, suggestions and interest in my story. She has been an incredible resource and partner and has held my hand as a novice writer through this process. Without her, my book would not have become a reality and I am forever grateful to have met her and chosen her for my book.

I am forever grateful for my parents for the sacrifices they made to afford their children better opportunities in life and for the values they instilled in us, such as the importance of family, integrity, kindness, compassion, the value of education, work ethics, responsibility, consciousness and generosity. They raised us to be confident, resilient and resourceful. I know they are watching over us, they are proud of us and they love us.

My sisters were my big sisters and my role models all my life and despite all three of us being very different in some ways, we have a strong sense of sisterhood, family, love and support. I am so fortunate to have had their love and support throughout my life. Even through some of the most difficult and challenging points in my life, they were always there for me. I am blessed to have them in my life and now with my parents gone, they mean even more to me. I am looking forward to our golden years and a different level of closeness and love we will share as our family grows.

I have learned so much from people I have loved, loved and lost, and continue to love. Some taught me about unconditional love, some taught me not to settle out of fear, some taught me that life without passion is fatal, and some taught me that being kind is more important than being right. Some taught me that no matter how much you love someone and the environment you create for them, you cannot change them. Some taught me (as Gabriel Garcia Marquez said) that you are never too old to fall in love, it's only when you stop loving that you get old. Some taught me that it's OK to let go and let others do things for you, some taught me that if they are not asking for help, don't try to fix things, you need to let it be. Most of all, they all taught me that there is nothing more powerful than love.

I have some amazing friends who have been there for me for a season, for a reason or for life and have broadened my views, inspired me and challenged me when needed. They have loved, encouraged and supported me through my life's journey and have always, always, always been there for me. I cherish my friendships and I know that they will always be part of my journey.

My son has been the bright and shining light in my life and the reason for my strength in my ability to continue to love life despite my circumstances. He is the reason I can truly practice that 10%

is what happens to you in life and 90% is how you respond to it. He has given me the opportunity to see life through a different lens. He has taught me about deep compassion even for strangers, infinite love, kindness and genuine interest in each and every person and boundless curiosity about the world in general. He has also tested my patience more than a few times as though he knew that working on my patience was one of my life's works and although it has helped, it still needs a lot of work on my part. Of course I love my son because he is my son, but I am happy that I like him for the person he is. I look up to him and I continue to learn from him. He is an old soul and I am thankful for the amazing connection we have at a very deep level.

Finally, I am grateful for the universe and all that it has presented me with throughout my life. I am grateful for it knowing exactly what I needed and when, and what I couldn't handle. It continues to amaze me with all the magic that life itself presents. Keep bringing it on. If you remember anything of me, after I leave this world, remember that I loved even when it was foolish and that I cared, even when it was unwanted. When my body is gone, remember my heart and soul.

Life Without Love is No Life at All — Leonardo Da Vinci